E.M.S.R.P.

UNFREEZING THE AUTHENTIC SELF

Reclaiming the Potential

Your Upbringing Put Out of Reach

Mac Andrews

E.M.S.R.P. UNFREEZING THE FROZEN AUTHENTIC SELF

Copyright © 2014 by (Mac Andrews aka Andrew McCamley)

ISBN-13: 978-1500341695
ISBN-10: 150034169X

Dedication

With special thanks and love to all of the participants who over the years have contributed to the fabric of this powerful process especially those from the Actors Institute UK and the Institute for Creativity, men and women who completed the One Year Leadership Programme with me and the pioneering individuals across the globe who have transformed their lives using this process and trusted me to facilitate them as they did so.

My thanks also go to Steve Harold who was the first therapist to use this process from end to end and achieve fantastic results with his clients, for the faith he showed in me in so doing and his choice to accompany me on this exciting journey.

My wife Kim and my children, Abbie and Jessica, deserve my deepest gratitude for living this process with me, and for being the evidence of what is possible when the developmental process is given the most nurturing environment to continue its natural course. Your love and support, your simple being of your essence, the amazing human beings you each are have all fed my courage on this adventure. Thanks for being such major contributors to my personal thriving and that of EMSRP.

Table of Contents

Foreword

It is not often you meet someone who makes such a big difference to your life and to so many people around you including loved ones and strangers. Mac Andrews is one of those rare breeds whose integrity and insight make you feel immediately respected, and that anything is possible. I have known Mac for over 25 years and am privileged to be able to call him a dear friend.

Over those years and more he has used his skills, insights and experience from a unique career path combining acting, directing, marketing research and psychology. From his acting career he discovered that you must be willing to take the lid off deep emotions and shameful beliefs in order to own all that you are. Mac learnt that even within the same script, unique performances are possible if you live more in the moment and are willing to go with the flow of that moment. From this he became more curious about those deeper forces within himself and others, and how they influenced behaviours and life choices, such as career and personal relationships.

He discovered that most people have a core negative belief about themselves that limits their life choices and often makes them settle for less. He started putting together therapeutic processes to assist people who were going through difficult times with their career, marriage or those that felt stuck, trapped and unhappy.

During this time he often described to me the way he was working and the results he was getting. As a hypnotherapist I am always looking for more tools to add to my toolbox. I would sometimes try out Mac's processes and found them to be highly effective.

Mac is one of those uncommon people who seems to be able to get in touch with what is going on for anyone in difficulty and help them find a way through. He is a man of amazing courage who despite having his own fears, doesn't let them get in the way of his thriving. So it was very flattering to be invited by Mac to become involved with helping people using his approach, which he has called EMSRP – Expressive Meta-Schematic Re-Patterning.

Naturally both of us wanted to know whether Mac's spectacular EMSRP results were unique to him, or repeatable by a different practitioner. A couple of years ago I started offering EMSRP in my therapy practice and it was highly satisfying for me to duplicate the results Mac has been achieving. I also found that on a personal level just reading about the 7 steps in EMSRP changed me, or should I say, *freed* me from some of my limitations.

I know that one of Mac's dreams is to leave a legacy. When I consider just a few of the areas EMSRP could help such as depression, self esteem, career choice, mid-life crisis, healthy parenting, children and teenage, and old age thriving, I have no doubt that Mac is making his dream a living reality and I am very excited to play some part in it all.

Steven Harold

Preface

The world is full of therapies. Why on Earth would a new one contribute anything? It's everywhere already. Workshops, one-to-one, life coaching, encounter groups, religious and spiritual practices, self-help books – surely if there's an answer to the woes of the flesh it's out there. It is...probably...but I could never find it all in one place. Each time I tried some new approach that promised the world I noticed my excitement rise, a thrilling upsurge of hope for change. Each time I found myself back in my life experiencing many of the same patterns that had led me to seek help in the first place. It would be unfair to claim that nothing changed, some things did, but not enough changed to satisfy me. I was desperate to get there, wherever "there" was, but again and again I discovered that I was simply never even nearly...well, there. Every approach seemed to demand ruthless discipline I could never quite muster, blind and frameless faith that seemed to disaappoint or the need to keep on returning for costly 'top ups' or endless menus of 'advanced courses'.

My journey through to the construction of Expressive Meta-Schematic Re-Patterning (EMSRP) was, in its first iteration, a huge experiment inside the laboratory of my own life. I have blundered, blubbed and battered my way through a multitude of approaches, and although each made its various sized incremental contribution, none gave me a whole, practical understanding for this thing called" life" and my place in it. It has to be said that to one extent or another each in its own way was necessary, but no one perspective was sufficient. A sort of 'one-stop-process' was what I sought and EMSRP emerged by default to fill the gap

To introduce you to EMSRP I think you deserve to know how it came about in its present form.

I started out as a professional actor. Acting saved my life. I could do it well enough to win some admiration in a school system through the 1960's that had terrified me out of striving in anything academic. Sport was rough, tough, rugby-playing violence and my cowardice soon closed off that route to achievement in any meaningful way.

To describe the culture simply, teachers beat students and students beat students; the beaten students then beat both each other and themselves in a perfect storm of shaming. We were beaten by each other's competition emotionally, psychologically and especially physically. Being pretty low in the hierarchy I became much beaten by it with few opportunities to do any beating for myself, ironically itself a situation I beat myself for mercilessly.

Drama was not on the curriculum and thus was not rated very highly; it involved none of the normal punishing expectations attached to everything else and so for the most part it escaped the violence. I slid in there for relief, and discovered inside a creative freedom that paved my way out of hell. While everyone else agonized about the expected university place for those who could, or a life in banking or insurance for those who couldn't, I quietly auditioned for, and was accepted by a leading drama school – and this marked a life-saving turning point.

On my journey through acting training I discovered that there are, broadly speaking, two types of actors. First, there are those who do *impressions* of human experience and character, without any immersion in any kind of real internal human experience. In fact many of this type of actor even pride themselves on being able to plan their weekly shopping whilst 'giving their' Macbeth or Aladdin. They lie to *appear* truthful. They are Masters of Disguise. You will know them; when required to cry they force themselves to refrain from blinking until their eyes sting and their eyelids quiver as they resist the blink reflex sufficiently long to produce a tear. Somehow, they never *move* the audience to their own inner emotional experience. The second type strike a stark contrast; they are those actors who have delved so deeply into their inner psyche that they can wear their make-believe lives like real life itself, responding to the script, other characters and imaginary surroundings with total integrity – they *are* Macbeth or Aladdin. Their tears are sourced in true grief even though the situation is a witnessed fiction. They tell a profound emotional truth even though it is in service to the lie, the fictitious story they participate in telling. They are the Masters of Self.

One of the great benefits to the latter, the Master of the Self, is that no secrets, no taboos, are off limits; indeed the areas of experience that normal humans would shun and take great pains to avoid, are priceless resources to such artists. Actors in search of Mastery of the Self uncover their dark secrets with enthused relish knowing that they form a crucial part of the truth of human existence and experience, all to the benefit of their craft as sculptors of madness. They put to good use the abuses and traumas of their past, allowing them to be witnessed by faceless audiences and leaving catharsis in their wakes. They permit the ticket paying punters to peep through the keyhole at covert aspects of human experience held tightly secret in normal culture, and for their witnesses to heal a little, to 'live' the moments with them. Macbeth as a disguise, a hollow pretense, serves the audience little in his travels through the taboo-busting ambition that Shakespeare's title character is forced to endure. The spoken verse may impress, but the play will not reveal its profound inner depths when simply performed as a technical exercise.

Macbeth as a journey through genuine, tormented, conflicted self-revelation is an entirely different experience – an audience is invited into the discomfiting presence of their own capacities for fear, grief, greed, sexual dependency, the terrifying capacity of all human beings to rationalise their abuses of others in service to ruthless ambition, indeed their madness and that of Macbeth.

Training actors, directing and acting in pursuit of my own aspirations towards mastery of the self (whilst I make no claim to have achieved this in all respects) fundamentally altered me, my students and fellow actors in ways that resulted in unexpected bonuses in the form of transformative life changes. At this point I have to say that most if not all of the actors in pursuit of mastery that I met, and I include myself in this, were drawn to the art out of personal dysfunction of one type or another. Speaking solely for myself, I could not sustain loving relationships, was filled with fear of life, experienced massive dips and peaks of self worth, was subject to deep convictions of non-belonging, profound undeserving, flawedness, was sexually promiscuous, and yet I still felt compelled to parade myself before audiences risking their rejection for what they saw in me. Flirting with the yawning threat of "being found out" I found myself in good company amongst actors and performers of all kinds who suffered the same terrible agonies of self-doubt and terror, each of us learning to operate in spite of the inner pain and calling this unutterable torment "art". Suffering and art were assumed to go hand in hand, something I know now is not the case at all, and that fascinated me. It is, I now know, simply a justificatory myth.

The human capacity to endure suffering even in the face of kinder alternatives has always intrigued me. Shamed by paralyzing secrets I noticed that others had the same paralyzing secrets that drove their compulsive social pretenses, their smoke-screen behaviours and even whole identities, just as they were driving mine. We were *formed* out of our most shameful secrets. Once shared however, these secrets lost their power to paralyze. Once harnessed for creative expression before audiences their grip was removed and they became both transformed and transformational. The reclaimed secret became a resource for creative expression – the person became the master able to create forms *with* the secret rather than continuing to be formed *by* it. The implications of this insight alone in EMSRP are profound.

My approach to training became a hungry campaign to drive more, indeed *all* of these secrets to the surface; all and everything was made welcome, taboos, crimes, weaknesses, abuses both suffered and perpetrated, all were put into the communal melting pot. Their fullest creative expressions were then staged or filmed or both, their emotions channeled into theatre of all sorts, witnessed and riotously applauded. Through this process catharsis felt complete. There was forgiveness, acceptance, inclusion, balance restored to each and every person, for self and each other. There was grounded bliss in it.

Experienced professionals and young aspiring artists queued for classes called *"Owning Your Inner Ugly"*, *"Transcending Abuse"*, *"Creating From Shame"*; we ran *"Sex Days"* and *"Madness Days"*. We, collectively, increasingly thrived.

I plundered every therapy and discipline I could find for ways to penetrate to the inner reaches of the most disowned parts of self, to befriend them and invite their participation in creative self-expression towards the art of acting at its deepest and most powerful. We instituted ethics designed to keep people safe from *actual* abuses as we powered through our subterranean selves.

Bit by bit others arrived wanting some of what we were doing – therapists, accountants, executives, unemployed, depressed, lonely, lost, poor and wealthy alike. Bit by bit my body of work became a leadership course.

We were onto something, but I noticed that with non-actors I had a background feeling of unease about the method's impacts on their relationships with the real world they returned to inhabiting after our encounters. For people outside the expressive arts, something was missing. For them the process was an act of faith – it had no robust theoretical basis, no integrated framework of understanding, no path for including what they had discovered into their day to day lives without causing massive disruption.

For Actors it had intuitive usefulness. Each fragment of self-forgiveness resulted in greater power to land acting work, increased presence on stage or in front of the camera and was accompanied by an irresistible sense of personal growth in life. For people in more practical life-roles, self-forgiveness and growing personal power felt great in the carefully engineered, safe and ethical contexts we collectively constructed to nurture our 'dangerous' journeys together. Thrust back into the unchanged constraints of ordinary life however, it was left to our non-actors to incorporate their newly uncovered powers into the narrow boundaries of the jobs, the marriages, the social groups that formed the fields of play for their everyday lives. They were left emotionally and psychologically incontinent, much bigger people than their legacy relationships were able to contain – strangers in the worlds they had previously created out of their relatively smaller size. Unlike the actors, they had no framework for understanding what had happened and how it could be used to benefit their real lives. They were set loose with bigger engines than their driving ability could manage, pedal to the metal, on roads that had little room for mistakes and with too little expertise. Their mistakes simply succeeded in reaffirming their worst self images; I met many people who when being frankly honest would say, "I am afraid that nothing works for me, there is simply something wrong with me…there must be."

It became dazzlingly obvious to me that this approach was missing crucial pathways to ease the newly awakened person into their real world. Each participant needed simple ways to reintroduce gradually their developmentally reawakening self into the still-frozen and unchanged world. The programme lacked assignments that allowed them to rehearse and explore themselves thoroughly without blowing everything that was of value to them to smithereens or requiring them to squeeze their growing size back into the 'shoes' left outside the door and now too small. It needed an ethical, philosophical and methodological framework that respected the others in their lives who had not been there to grow too, and processes that allowed *them* to encounter this newly growing participant, without being rendered terrified, made to feel wrong, less, expected to 'grow' too.

It additionally needed a rational even scientific framework that promoted full understanding of the causes of the change they were experiencing, as well as scripts for conversations that might enable them to describe and explain it to people who had not been at its inception. It needed to make sense at all levels, not simply to be a brilliant, explosive, life-changing experience that could not be incorporated into making life feel better, everywhere. After all, friends, family, lovers were not an audience waiting to applaud. There was a great deal at stake for them as well. For those non-acting brethren, our actors' processes needed substantial reinvention.

So that is what I worked on and how EMSRP came into being nearly two decades ago.

I stopped acting and training actors soon after my first daughter was born. I felt compelled to provide for my family, and to be at home rather than forever touring, so I used my knowledge to create an international research consultancy to provide insights to businesses and food on our table. This left me room, alongside being a DAD, to review my work, to do a formal honours degree in Psychology and to conduct an organised and rigorous study of each of the processes of EMSRP with individual participants. Thus I began to explore the most powerful, ethical and relevant ways to help people unstick their stuckness, and to make better ways stick rather than depend on constant returning to 'groups' or 'workshops' in the constant cycle of feeding and depletion that I see all too often in other therapeutic communities. I invited people with depression and stuckness to participate in my study for free, and they paid me with their data. Their lives changed quickly, radically, beneficially and so did their worlds around them.

Once sufficiently certain through data collection, research and revision that this had become a reliable, responsible and effective process, I had to find out if it could be facilitated equally effectively by another person. My beloved friend and colleague Steven Harold, a Clinical Hypnotherapist, generously took on the process, and from my written explanation of philosophy, methodology and method, he invited participants to participate with him with equally powerful results.

Through case references the evidence for the effectiveness of the process is shared throughout this book. We do not claim that this powerful process that will suit and be effective for everyone. We do, however, often sit together open mouthed at the extraordinary, speedy and beneficial shifts that all people who do it report to us as they complete each step. We watch too as we both thrive and grow, and see those around us thriving and growing too. The shifts have longevity as they are embodied in the participant.

We want to share this. For me, it is my legacy, my life's work thus far. It expresses who I am and what I am for at my quintessential best. I do not claim enlightenment, far from it, but thanks to this journey I have a life with people I love and who thrive with me, who grow through the simple principles of this work in the course of life, not as a discipline, but through being themselves emerging out of present circumstances, not entrapment in unconsciously recycled behaviours dictated from the past. I find myself in a real life that I love with real people that I love and it is this process that is the distillation of everything that has made that possible, probable, actually in all honesty a process that is designed to make it inevitable.

The framework is robust, the steps make sense in an order that ensures change. We know so many programmes promise change – this process lays stages in a logical progression that *causes* each participant to *cause* change in and around themselves. Each assignment takes what is learned into the laboratory of life itself – so each step is proven in real life before the next step is commenced. EMSRP weaves each participant's genuine inner world into their outer world piece by piece until the real person can start to grow uninhibited again in interdependent relationships that support rather than obstruct their fundamental drive to express their own unique essence into the world. Nothing in EMSRP cultivates dependency on the facilitator. It has a beginning, a middle, and *especially* an end.

We are privileged and excited to be the authors and guardians of the process.

To grow it must be shared – we want to share it.

Introduction

Expressive Meta-Schematic Re-Patterning (EMSRP) sounds like an awfully grand and technical name for a process claiming to help people unstick their 'stuckness'. People could get stuck trying to get their heads around the title alone! In fact the name is constructed to represent a high level overview of what the process is and how it works. It emerged to describe, in as pithy a way as possible, a seven step series of experiences and their results that takes between 6 months and a year to complete. One short phrase cannot contain all that it entails. Nonetheless, the name on the tin describes exactly what its contents do, and to explain this I will deconstruct it word by word.

EMSRP is **EXPRESSIVE**. There is a saying in the world of 'Growth workshops' and therapy, *"It's easy to become great at therapy and lousy at life"*. EMSRP is designed to eliminate this tendency entirely. The process is comprised of steps that involve learning through insight. Insight is marked by those moments that suddenly cause you to gasp and say, *"I never realised that before – that changes everything."* Insight can be a shock or a relief. It can leave you feeling stupid, *"Why on earth didn't I see that before?"* or profoundly better informed, *"Oh, that's why!"* It rocks your world for a while because it calls for the re-examination of almost everything you thought you knew. As one of my participants recently observed, *"I feel like I took a blue pill and have seen the Matrix."* An insight is a powerful intrusion of a contradictory or illuminating 'truth'. We feel insight in our bodies first, without words to express it fully as it has not yet acquired the language needed. This leaves us a bit exposed for a time, like a naïve beginner, interrupted in our certainty that we were already masters.

Powerful as they are, insights can be swept back under the carpet without taking any action whatsoever. As Winston Churchill said, *"Occasionally men stumble over the truth, but most of them pick themselves up and hurry off as if nothing ever happened."* To ensure that every 'truth' is fully explored and implemented, the insights driven to the surface in each EMSRP session are put into action through simple assignments. These are designed to implement what is learned in simple and accessible ways within the fabric life itself, not as difficult disciplines or repeated practice, but through calculated, habit-breaking shifts in behaviour. Each assignment is, in effect, a short experiment designed to cause different results. Results are brought back to and reviewed in the following EMSRP session. This sequence of events mirrors directly how we learned as infants. We experimented until we discovered how to make the world work for us as best we could, given our own limitations and the conditions we found ourselves in. Experiments tend to be affected deeply by what we already believe we will find. The conditions of our lives changed over time, but the conclusions we drew from our earliest experiences soon coloured all our ensuing experiments. A child of 18 months knocked over by a wave 40 centimetres high on the seashore might wind up fearing the sea forever. Although they grow into a tall adult, the internal conception of the wave proportionally grows with them. The original wave may have been two feet high, but to the adult it might feel two meters tall.

Each assignment is a new experiment driven by fully understood insight – the results are quickly very compelling. What is learned is soon surprisingly **expressed automatically** in the real world.

This is because EMSRP works at a **Meta-Schematic** level. We are driven to behave by beliefs. The most powerful beliefs dictating our behaviours lie beyond our conscious awareness because they were formed before we could speak or even remember specific events on our lives. They were learned in the same way that we learned to catch a ball or ride a bike. They are *procedural beliefs* that formed before we could lay down conscious, retrievable memories of events in our lives (about 30 months in neurotypical humans). These procedural beliefs were then schematised, i.e. translated into blueprint, unconsciously planned behaviours that continue to dominate us in later life. Some behaviours are useful, necessary even, but others impose themselves and defeat our yearnings to do things differently, spoiling life and trapping us in patterns of unwanted behaviour we seem unable to do much about. We are even painfully aware of what we do, when and how and yet still we cannot sustainably change. We are left saying things like, *"That's just me"*. That promise, *"I'll change"* has a hollow ring. The Meta-Schematic belief is the super belief, the belief of beliefs, that cheats us from growing and developing into the person we secretly suspect we could have been *"if only..."*. It leads us into stuckness, depression, and frustrated repetition of our own self-defeating habits and our self-surrender to the effects of negative behaviours from others. In EMSRP this belief and all attached behaviours are surfaced, explored and understood. It is a revelation, always. The transformation is Meta-Schematic too affecting all aspects of life for the better. Change is inevitable and takes participants by surprise when they find they are behaving quite differently in circumstances that previously would have led to self-defeating or undesirable default responses. That is radical and brings us to the final word in its title.

EMSRP is a process of **Re-Patterning**. This is perhaps the most inadequate term in the title. It is widely agreed across developmental psychology that at birth every child embodies an innate drive to develop well, and to continue developing to their fullest extent. This natural urge can be thwarted, redirected or invalidated as they interact with the permissions and constraints within their environment and the people who are part of it.

The human entity senses stimuli that have an effect upon them. This effect invites a response that leads to expression in the form of behaviour. In turn, the behaviour causes consequential outcomes in the environment, and these outcomes result in the formation of beliefs.

Here's an example of a **supportive** cycle:-

COLD (environmental stimulus) –

FEAR (effect) –

PHSYIOLOGICAL IMPULSE (response) –

CRYING (expression) –

CARE AND ATTENTION LEADING TO INCREASED WARMTH (consequential outcome) –

"WHEN I CRY FROM COLD I RECEIVE INCREASED WARMTH" (belief).

Here is an **obstructive** cycle:-

INSECURE (stimulus) –

FEAR (effect) –

PHYSIOLOGICAL IMPULSE (response) –

SHOUTING WITH ANGER (expression) –

PUNISHMENT AND THREATS OF ABANDONMENT (outcome) -

ANGER IS BAD AND THREATENS MY LIFE (belief)

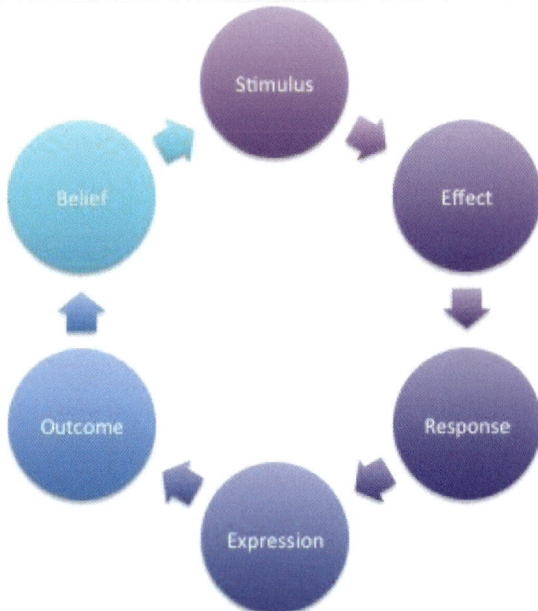

This dynamic of stimulus-effect-response-behaviour-outcome-belief results in pre-verbal behavioural patterns becoming reinforced by inner, unconscious, unspoken belief systems that quickly freeze important aspects of development. This frozen authentic *potential* becomes trapped inside patterns of behavior that prevent and frustrate further development in all sorts of subtle and significant ways.

EMSRP creates the conditions for the reawakening of _all_ of the halted developmental processes and by means of careful re-parenting (by the participant and modeled by the facilitator) brings the postponed potential self into mature expression. Thoroughly preparing the ground for such a huge endeavour is vital. That is why the early stages are particularly rich with insight and personal shifts — preparation for the day when each participant's life is emancipated from the meta-schematic belief's limits and into their care. Arguably, it could be called Expressive Meta-Schematic Re-*Parenting*. But the patterns that change life outcomes go way beyond the fundamental requirement of re-parenting the emerging, blossoming authentic self and its unique character that we call ESSENCE.

After the first session, each subsequent meeting begins with the question, *"What is different?"* Focusing on what is changing in life and evaluating what each shift makes possible for the participant that was not possible prior to it is pivotally important. Evolutionary psychology tells us that one of the ways cultures alter is when new behaviours are modeled and adopted by others in social settings. It is from preferable outcomes to carefully targeted, pattern-interrupting behaviours that new behaviours take root and flourish. Knowing why and how these simple new behaviours work and what they deliver from the environment helps them stick and become repeatable without effort, and ultimately without thought.

Sometimes small changes in behaviour profoundly alter long-term outcomes in totally unforeseeable ways. We can find ourselves somewhere totally unexpected when we simply turn left rather than habitually turning to the right. It is known now that for our mental health we need to possess a coherent autobiographical narrative in order to make sense of ourselves in the world in which we find ourselves. One of the insights underlying current understanding of Post Traumatic Stress Disorder is that overwhelming and uninvited events that do not fit into our coherent self-story can intrude repeatedly and unannounced into consciousness long after the actual event itself has passed, totally overwhelming and hijacking our awareness in the present; this can cause sufferers to lose total cognizance of who and where they are, and to behave as if the intruding reality from the past is absolute reality in the present moment. For soldiers from war zones it is obvious how debilitating and dangerous PTSD can be. Understanding how you arrive at an unexpected destination, as well as *who you are* in it, are both critical pieces of knowledge for a coherent narrative for the newly re-developing self to be constructed. Arriving somewhere without any sense of a journey to get there is potentially traumatic. EMSRP only goes forward at a rate that each individual participant's understanding can sustain. Seeing what is different and knowing what it was each participant has done to contribute to the change matters a great deal, and thus the question, *"What is different?"*, though strange at first, quickly finds a central role in the successful EMSRP journey.

So there you have it, **Expressive** (in the world) **Meta-Schematic** (behaviour driving belief) **Re-Patterning** (Re-schematising through safe, stepped and simple behavioural breakthroughs).

EMSRP is *not* about recycling the past. Although the stories of the past may be useful, they are not the primary focus of the process. We are called to notice the 'me' and its 'world' in the present. There are certain processes that involve exploring specific past situations; these are purposeful journeys to resource practical assignments in the world of the present that drive important breakthroughs. Sometimes association with the past are made as insights about how a thriving environment might work land with an accompanying "aha" moment.

These past associations can be very useful indeed, and may occur with the need to grieve for a while or to experience a sense of relief.

The sessions follow a pattern:-

1. Observed changes resulting from experimental assignments and their implications for thriving,
2. New thinking with a full explanation,
3. Experiential 'presencing' work of the insight through games/techniques/processes
4. Assignment(s) to further presence the insight and/or to take it into a live social setting

Only when the assignments for a preceding step have been completed can the following step begin. A step may take as many as four sessions, or may be completed across one plus the assignment time leading up to the following meeting. Individual participants take as long as they need to fully integrate what they learn.

Some participants do a step and then leave for a while. They then return to the next when and if they feel ready. This has proven to be quite effective for some, although there can be a tendency to lose momentum and fall away from the programme. Our ethics dictate that people can leave whenever they want – this is a process rooted in mutual consent based on full knowledge, thus there are, and must be no secrets. People can withdraw as and when they wish without any coercion or explanation. No freedoms are surrendered at all in entering this process with a facilitator. All of the rights and ethics are fully explained in a form in the first session, the contents of the form are discussed and then signed once the participant decides to pursue the programme.

Data are collected for the first time after the first session when the full programme and its principles have been outlined, considered and a period of two weeks has elapsed for participants (however keen or urgently they want to proceed) to think through the implications of the work. Once they have signed the awareness form, the first data sheet can be filled in. This consists of self-scoring against 26 key indicators of depression. The use of depression as a broad indicator for progress in EMSRP is informed by the conviction that ease of flow of essence into the external world is marked by the absence of symptoms of depression, and obstructed flow marked by depressive symptoms. Over the years this has provided a clear progress marker for the programme and aided its improvement in increasing progress scores. A total of four readings are taken at specific stages. All data are held and once included in the growing data set are rendered anonymous.

The first data are taken prior to step 2. The second are taken after the Bill of Rights has been constructed and put into a formal document.

The third are taken upon completion of the FInal step.

The final reading is taken 12 months after the programme has formally ended. This enables us to find out if the effects are lasting, stable or improving.

Of course with any programme involving work over a period of months, it can be argued with some merit that any life changes could be due to other intervening factors in a person's life. We cannot contest this point of view with an absolute causal claim. However the dat are compelling. People come to the programme with symptoms of life-stuckness, often after trying one or a series of therapeutic solutions. They take an inner reading of the strength of these symptoms at the beginning. The second reading indicates a 35-70% fall in strength of symptoms. In work with depression you can commonly find that once a person begins to talk about their experience with another concerned individual, a drop in symptomatic strength is likely. The size of the effect in EMSRP is what is most impressive. Additionally the symptom strength drops further at the third reading, and we are finding that a year later these low scores have remained relatively stable or have dropped further. Of course EMSRP engineers the shift in life events that support lower scores through the assignments, many of which require

21

deliberate and calculated social pattern changes. Shifting behaviours alone would have little longevity; we have all been on failed diets for example. The behaviour alterations are conducted concurrently with radical changes in relationship with the Meta-Schematic Belief and all of its psychological and behavioural compulsions. Behaviour changes *emerge unexpectedly* as clients go about their normal business. Changes in response, thought and action embed themselves unnoticed and cause different consequential outcomes. The changes are far reaching – and they receive conscious support rather than unconscious resistance through the opening minutes of each session.

Some, if not all of the processes are not entirely unique. I think that I invented some of them, but in the realm of personal exploration many people have developed all sorts of clever methods for deep diving into the sea of the inner self. I am indebted to all of the programs, workshops, disciplines, therapies, philosophies, psychological perspectives both mainstream and alternative, and even some religious philosophies for elements that have made contributions to the unique configuration of principles and processes that comprise EMSRP. It is in its whole model of human social development from infant to adult, and the dynamic interaction between each participant and their internal and social realities that it finds its full potency to bring about individual thriving to replace unease, dysfunction and depression.

In order to describe EMSRP in such a way that others may develop the fullest grasp of its psychology, philosophy, methodology and methods available without undergoing the process itself with a qualified and licensed practitioner, I have outlined the whole programme in detail. Each step is exposed following a series of written events.

1. The purpose of the step and its importance are explored and described. Over the course of the entire handbook a psychology, or psychologies, and philosophical framework emerge.

2. A full participant-centred explanation for the step is included, as well as some of the issues that might emerge before a participant

and their facilitator are explored in some depth (e.g. procrastination, resistance, defences, doubts etc).

3. Example questions and interaction techniques for eliciting the desired psychological material from within each participant to work with throughout the session and in their 'homework' assignments.

4. Any forms, insight and assignment aids for the use of the facilitator and/or participant that we use are presented, outlined and explained.

5. Some of the typical challenges arising from each step are illustrated with a selection of case study samples.

6. Practical assignments for participants are fully explained and scripted to further outline how they are delivered, what they are for, timescales for completion alongside examples of learning that they typically deliver.

7. Each step must be completed before moving on. The conditions for completion are described.

The Legal and Ethical Bit

We have to stress that EMSRP dives deeply into emotional and psychological material in a responsible and strictly ethical way. It is facilitated by fully qualified, accredited and trained people each of whom has undergone and completed the whole EMSRP program and accreditation. They have fulfilled the requirements of EMSRP.org before being given permission to offer our programme to their clients with our fully informed blessing. If you attempt any of the processes on your own behalf you do so at your own risk and EMSRP.org can accept no liability for any adverse results you experience. To use the techniques described within this book in part or in whole with others, taking on the role of facilitator on their behalf without accreditation by EMSRP.org is not advisable. To adopt or claim the letters *EMSRP* or *Expressive Meta Schematic Re-Patterning* (or *Expressive Meta-Schematic Re-Parenting*) and offer EMSRP as a form of therapeutic intervention, counselling, life-coaching or group work of any kind without accreditation training and qualification approved by EMSRP.org, as well as being ill advised and potentially harmful to both facilitator and participant, is also a breach of copyright and misuse of intellectual property owned exclusively by Mac Andrews and EMSRP.org.

Chapter One

Fully Informed Consent.

AIMS AND OBJECTIVES.

The aim of Step One is to empower the *potential* participant in giving or withholding **fully informed consent** to participation in the whole programme, to understand the extent of their ethical rights and to experience mindfully, probably for the first time in their lives, what it takes to construct a healthy and supportive relationship. Treating yourself and your needs as priorities in the construction of relationships designed to support thriving in life represents a core range of skills to be developed and reinforced throughout the seven steps. *Needs* are a central concern. Most people have been raised to live in bad faith with their needs, suppressing them, redirecting them, ignoring them even abusing themselves for them. Step 3 focuses on the identification of a range of unconscious unmet needs and exploring the creation of relationships within which they could be exposed, accepted, communicated and met. The very beginnings of the relationship with any new participant must be fully constructed to take care of needs many of which the participant will inevitably be unaware even exist for them. Modeling the construction of a healthy relationship must be mindfully done, even and especially with participants who are overtly keen to get going as soon as they can.

People who seek help through EMSRP are almost certainly out of touch with their needs, and are likely to be unable to create and sustain relationships within which they can thrive. They are also likely therefore, to lack a sufficient sense of their own value and importance. They are often looking for someone else to take responsibility for their safety, wellbeing and happiness and unconsciously living in hope of rescue.

This preparatory step (Step One) ensures that the prospective participant is taken through a thorough examination of the implications of this level of work for them. They may be used to being bullied, accepting abuse, allowing others to make their choices for them, and/or making reckless and unconsidered decisions, they may even expect that you as the facilitator will do the process for them; they may hope for/fear a sexual relationship with you enmeshed with a host of unmet, undeclared and unconscious hungers that will, should they proceed, be thoroughly surfaced and addressed through the programme. Therefore before they embark on the EMSRP programme, the facilitator takes them painstakingly through a full description of the background, philosophy and processes involved, and considers at a surface level how it relates to their experience of life, it takes them through consideration of each aspect of the *"Awareness Form"* (appendix 1) and then affords them a two-week 'cooling off' period. They are reassured that after their cooling off period it will be absolutely fine for them to refuse to continue and that the facilitator will harbour no ill will towards them at all, and no time will have been wasted. This demonstrates the construction of healthy foundations that could support the building of a healthy relationship, one designed for them to be able to feel safe, and ultimately one dedicated to the thriving of both participant and facilitator. It is likely to be the first time they will have experienced this level of consideration at this stage of any relationship, ever.

- EMSRP requires a high level of sustained commitment.
- Each step may take several sessions to complete.
- Their feeling states will move up or down throughout the process.
- They may find parts of the programme confusing or even distressing.

- They may find that they may experience depressive symptoms that may vary in intensity throughout the process.
- If they become suicidal or self-destructive then they are required to make a clear agreement to contact the facilitator at specified times, or failing that, if they have one, their therapist or counsellor, or to contact the Samaritans and admit to the truth of their thoughts, feelings and experience to the telephone volunteer if the facilitator or therapist are not available.
- As the participant changes, their changes will have impacts on relationships within social, professional and familial spheres; EMSRP is designed to facilitate the changing participant in introducing their newly developing self to their pre-existing personal social world in graduated steps, and whilst some of these relationships may readily accept the changes they meet, others may not support them.

What must also be explained?

1 Ethics:- These are enshrined in the Awareness Form that is attached as appendix 1. The Primary Governing Ethic is that no person abuses another. 'Abuse' is defined here as the use of one person for another's needs without their *full knowledge* and *consent*. This means that all aspects of the process must be fully explained with no secrets, no hidden agendas, no coercion and based on fully informed agreement to proceed. **Abuse threatens thriving always**; *non-abuse therefore must be an active practice* and wherever it is found to occur within the relationship between participant and facilitator, especially when perpetrated by the facilitator it must be admitted and the situation rectified. Non-abuse is a profound and difficult tenet to embody, and it is this that makes the work of the facilitator somewhat akin to an idealised priesthood. Sexualised or sexual relationship with any participant is assumed to be abusive at any time during or within five

years of completion of the programme, as the facilitator attains relatively greater power within the process compared to the participant. The dynamic is particularly acute between male heterosexual facilitators and women participants, and Peter Rutter's (1991) challenging book *Sex in the Forbidden Zone* provides an excellent account of how the inequities in power relations can spark powerful drives to abuse authority. It is recommended reading for anyone wanting to lead this work, and a vital text for accreditation.

      2 Process:- The process emerges out of its theoretical background. Describing the individual experiential sub-processes that participants will undertake and the assignments themselves will make little or no sense without the theory. Therefore this initial step requires that each process be described in the context of the theory.

      3) Awareness Form:- the form is attached as appendix 1.

The   Process – here is food for a script.

Every facilitator must develop their own script to take their clients through the process prior to their final consent to continue. The following explanation is thorough and written to provide them with the raw materials to construct the overview that most suits them and their client.

When you were born you could meet *none* of your own needs. You were totally dependent on others to meet any and all of your needs. Your higher thinking functions were not developed (your brain was years away from full size and development). Your eyes could not focus yet. You had no separate awareness of your own existence – i.e. you existed in the moment driven entirely by unthinking reflexes and instincts. You could not think about yourself, your actions, your thoughts or interpret events in the world.

You were, however, like all normally developed newborn infants PROGRAMMED TO SURVIVE.

Yet, you had no control over your own body and nothing to actively contribute to your own survival except to send out distress signals. Your life depended on being able to get help. Your needs could invade suddenly and getting someone to respond effectively and speedily to them was vital.

Your only language in this endeavour was a piercing cry to express your various and sometimes invisible needs - for reassuring contact with others, for nourishment, removal of acidic faeces and urine from your skin, attention to pain and temperature adjustment. Knowing that someone would come was essential to your growing confidence and trust.

If they didn't come, your instincts drove you to behave with increasing urgency, without conscious choice and purely as instinct.

So entire was your dependence on others **that abandonment was a threat to your survival**. This knowledge existed in your BEING not in your thoughts; it is an inheritance of our species, and perhaps all living creatures.

Abandonment meant death. The default in the very being of you as an organism was to avoid this at all costs.

You were not capable of thinking about this – it was, to all intents and purposes, **what you WERE**. So hard-wired into the psyche is this knowledge that adults can actually find themselves stating with absolute and passionate conviction, "Don't leave me or I'll die!" under threat of abandonment. This 'knowledge' is hardwired into us as a species; and wherever we believe our survival to be threatened, we automatically fight to survive.

Already as a newborn infant you were learning about whether or not it was safe for you to rely on other people. You learned this without conscious memory, language or reasoning. We know through extensive research that infants are incapable of recording retrievable memories until at least 30 months. So you learned these lessons about fundamental trust *procedurally*, like walking and grasping and releasing with your hands and arms. Your knowledge and the behaviours that the knowledge dictated became unconsciously automated and organized (schematized).

The needs your carer(s) noticed and responded to effectively legitimised those needs and also your expression of them; the ones they ignored, laughed at, barked angrily at or worse, punished, or abandoned you for were ones that you learned *procedurally* should be ignored, laughed at or punished, indeed abandoned – they were rendered *illegitimate* and recorded as dangerous. Some of your subtle needs were rendered illegitimate and yet, even so, they emerged inside you, they continued to impact on you, they craved expression into the outside world in the hope that they would be both noticed and responded to. Those needs unwanted by the world compelled you to 'unwant' them too. They became early evidence of parts of yourself that did not fit your world, were not welcome, were potentially dangerous to express to others and linked to potentially abandoning behaviours on the part of those you relied upon for your needs to be met. They threatened your belonging, safety and, yes, your survival. They taught you absolutely how to react to them – you learned to reject them absolutely.

Yet, **unfed the hungers persisted and persist to this day**. The crying may have been adequately hidden to the outside world but nonetheless, try as you might, it persisted inside.

Such needs became *secret* hungers.

Secret unacceptable hungers became very powerful indeed.

They continued and continue to try to find expression in the world, and they pop up to be noticed in all sorts of ways. In a sense, the crying child inside did not go away, and nobody bothered to pick it up and organise a way to meet his/her needs as they existed.

We have a saying in EMSRP – **"Chocolate will never hold you while you cry."** The subtle and destructive ways in which chronically unmet needs fuel countless self-defeating and baffling cycles of behaviour in the lives of each participant quickly become very clear in Steps 2 and 3 of the EMSRP programme.

It is important to realise that as a child you were not simply the receiver of good or bad care, a passive victim. As a child you were also an active participant – as we say in psychology, you had *'agency'*. You began to notice that you did things and they seemed to result in things happening as consequences – you acted on objects and people in your world, and they responded well, badly or did nothing. You noticed what won you the attention you needed and what failed. You noticed what caused threats and what invited support. As you progressed through infancy, you learned some absolute rules about your world, the objects and people in it and the extent and details of your power over them; you learned rules and formed beliefs even before you had language. You learned to know what you were, not through what you were told at first, but in the same way as you learned to catch a ball, or to walk. You did it by adjusting your behaviour until the required objectives were achieved, even if you had to settle for avoiding abandonment without the original need being met at all.

Survival is a *primary purpose*, before any supportive self-worth can be achieved preoccupation with survival is total. The avoidance of anything that might lead to abandonment when you were totally dependent was a pressing issue. Learning as a helpless, speechless being what it takes to survive is urgent business. Without trust in your environment to support you, then you are left unable to trust that support will be available on demand from the world you find yourself in. That world becomes a very dangerous place indeed. As you drew unreasoned conclusions about the many aspects of the world you experimented with, you also drew firm unreasoned conclusions about the nature of the sole common denominator – YOU. You, as a child, knew you were the cause of the effects around you, and the effects were your evidence to support your conclusions about your self. You learned what you deserved and what you did not, and from this you discerned who and what you were.

We are about to do a process where you learn to coax out the shamed and limited parts of yourself into the world, and then you are going to learn how to take care of this vulnerable part of yourself so he/she can play her part in the world as she truly is, and that the caretaking part of yourself can build relationships where he/she is safe to participate or withdraw, with a clear list of rights for thriving. You are going to take over being the best parent in the world to yourself, and this is going to transform your relationships so that you can create the circumstances for you to fulfill your self in the world and stop holding back."

On Shame and its Power.

There is a profound difference between allowing who you are – your unformed energy – to flow into the world without hindrance, spontaneously, adjusting to the changes in the environment as you go, rather like a surfer riding a wave, and entering a world anxious that you are about to be 'found out', exposed as flawed, shown up as wanting and inadequate, humiliated and embarrassed by the idea of someone seeing you as your most shaming belief about yourself. To negotiate a world where you fear exposure of your 'real-me' necessitates you having hyper-vigilant defenses, well and truly up and watching for external danger, whilst every-ready to stifle any dangerous internal impulses, and that you only operate those rigid and predictable life-formulae that you are sure will work to avoid exposure. Increasingly frequently, you were forced to behave in ways that were not 'natural' to you.

Out of these unnatural behaviours you constructed a sort of NON-SELF. The non-self's sole purpose became to obscure your REAL-SELF, with all its awkward, unacceptable and potentially dangerous needs. But the problem is that the REAL-SELF is where all your *authentic* feelings and impulses arise. Real feelings, real impulses are the authentic responses to the outside world FROM A REAL YOU. If these led to you being threatened, punished, humiliated, abandoned or ignored, then real feelings, real impulses became very dangerous indeed. You became the greatest threat to...*you*. The NON-SELF became a friend in need, a 'lifeboat' – it met the need to get by, to get just enough, but not and never to get authentic needs met. They had to be defused, redirected, blocked or eradicated or at the very urgent least, be successfully obscured from view.

The REAL-SELF became a secret and ashamed self. Real feelings therefore were clearly a product of the shamed REAL-SELF and thus they had to be held in check, hidden, smiled on top of, apologised for if they leaked out into the world where they could be witnessed by others. The sudden tears that are swallowed down and cause the friend to run from the room, the angry outburst followed by *"Look what you made me do – that's totally out of character with me!"*, or the constant reassertion *"I'm absolutely fine"* when you are clearly in pain and in need of medical assistance after a fall are all evidence of this toxic and self-alienating process in action.

We all learned to abandon and punish ourselves for essential parts of our innate human REAL powers, tools and resources. We all experienced our early authentic expressions meeting our environments, and because our environments existed within a bigger and more complex cultural system that embodied unclear rules about expression, we had to learn to behave in 'acceptable' ways, and in doing so we put our authentic selves away.

This, sadly, is ubiquitously normal. The Real or *Authentic* Self is almost always in whole or in significant part, rejected, condemned, criticised, punished and has become dangerous to us. And yet it is the *only* source of our emotions, our passions, our will, our desires, our vision, our genius, our charisma, our enthusiasm – without it everything must be dulled. The Non-self or as we will call it the *"not-me"* mask is like a false limb – it can have no blood running through it. So when the not-me meets someone else and real feelings emerge – the undeveloped, immature, frozen, rejected Authentic self gets thrown into the field of play with nobody to parent it, to make choices with it, to reassure it. It never gets to learn to walk. A four year old boy, incandescent with rage at his absent father and exhausted mother, forced to keep silent by the threat of punishment, unleashed into the adult body of the adult man who he grew up to be – a grown man raging with the skill of a four year old boy at a woman who comes home tired and irritable because her day has been so crappy, that man is very, very dangerous indeed. *"I'm so sorry, I'll never do it again. It was totally out of character with me,"* is never the answer.

The massive potential for a spacious and vibrant Authentic Self to develop and mature is quickly frozen, confined within strict and narrow boundaries and controlled as if it is the enemy. People often express their breakthroughs in terms of increased "space". As one participant in the early development of EMSRP said to me on discovering the sheer scale of the unfettered Authentic Self, *"It's like I am this house with multiple floors and hundreds of rooms – and I spent years in the downstairs toilet with the light off thinking that was all there was! I can't wait to throw open the windows and have a party in every room"*.

Shame drives hiding behaviours, hiding hijacks all of the person's inner powers in service to the deceit. It is exhausting and self-defeating and yet we have come to realise at EMSRP.org that it drives the world as we know it.

Show me someone who is over-performing and I will show you someone who is in flight from their authenticity. Yes, really, the flight from the frozen Authentic Self is that powerful.

So what is the purpose of shame?

Surely, if we have evolved with it, then it almost certainly must have a role in the success of our species.

Shame is about limits.

It is important to learn that you actually cannot fly without the aid of appropriate equipment, nor can you stop speeding buses with your soft human body like Superman, and fires will burn you no matter how much you practice putting your hand into naked flames. To all intents and purposes these limits are real.

But if you learn that when you feel physical or emotional pain, no matter how much you beg for help, nobody will listen *("Don't be such a wimp", "What is WRONG with you?", "You lack resilience")*, nobody will help you fathom how to make friends (*"It's your fault", "Why can't you be more like your brother?")*, nobody will accept your desires without you explaining yourself reasonably *("I want an ice cream"..."Why on Earth do you want an ice-cream?")*, nobody will approve of your innate perceptive ability *("Mum and Dad, are you quarrelling?"...."Of course not dear, we're absolutely fine sweetheart.")*, nobody loves you for being and expressing your anger, nobody accepts your imaginative interpretations of the world around you, *("When are you going to stop dreaming and get real?")*, when nobody will answer your need to play, *("Not now dear I'm busy, tired, talking, not interested, hate playing")*, nobody will respect your desire to shout "NO" to their invasion of your privacy (*"let Granddad kiss you", "You can't wash yourself")*, nobody lets you as a boy dress up as a girl, dance ballet, have dollies, wear pink, or as a girl they all disapprove if you want play with Action Man, wear trousers, make up, shout and scream, even worse nobody accepts the gender you are (*"I wanted a boy and you turned out to be a girl"),* when all of your attention is on the avoidance of the dangerous outburst that could occur at any moment from your drunken mother/father and the pleasing you will have to do to minimise their violence...

You learn about the impulses that emerge from deep inside the 'you' that you are from how they are received (welcomed, created with or frowned upon, ignored or punished). These build up a sense of limits that can become *toxically* shaming – they become limits that apply solely to YOU, and the impulses that emerge from YOU, the consequences that result from YOU expressing YOU.

And when we see that others seem able to receive, do, be and display the things that are forbidden to us, we get to feel different, comparatively flawed. We experience the effects of this relative deprivation – and we know with absolute certainty that this is because of who we ARE. Envy might tell us that we truly want what they have, and then we might find ways to construct it for ourselves. But the frozen Authentic Self leads to destructive jealousy: *"If I can't have it, then nobody should have it!"* I am struck by the numbers of women being subjected to horrific and disfiguring acid attacks at the moment of writing this perpetrated by rejected men – without doubt shame-driven behaviour.

This version of who we are forms a very powerful, secret and shaming belief – what we call a Meta-Schema. A Meta-Schema is an organised and organising belief on top of that all other self-beliefs (Sub-Schemata are founded – Schemata is the plural of Schema). We look for evidence to support such beliefs everywhere. The human mind is uniquely able to link cause and effect – it can link disease with invisible germs, connect flour, water and yeast with countless types of bread. However it can also link the sight of a comet with success in battle the following day. To the powerless the mind can read their shame into all sorts of outcomes that bear no direct relationship with reality. Shamed children know that they are the cause of their parents' divorce, illness, death, poverty. Their shame obsessively and compulsively drives responsibility for all that does not work, and their guilt becomes palpable.

Sometimes behaviour might invoke a catastrophic response – a one-off, sudden, paralyzing and overwhelming response from the world that sweeps away all sense of self and ends in abandonment, as in physical abuse and violence. This leaves the victim with the knowledge that catastrophic things can happen out of the blue that cancel out all sense of a self, things that overwhelm you with their power and against which there exists no possible defense. The child who is picked up violently, beaten and left alone learns that they are defenseless against danger. The message that, *"I only do it because I care"*, or *"it's because I love you that I..."* from the outside world makes a powerful association between the experience and the words "care" and "love" as shaming phenomena. *"I love you"* becomes wedded to violence, without which nurturing love becomes illegitimate. Violence and love become enmeshed in the sense of self. "All you need is love" takes on an entirely distorted meaning.

Imagine reaching out for an ice cream – you see it and imagine the cold, creamy, sweetness exploding in your hot, thirsty mouth. You grasp it in your hand. Nothing else exists to you except this ice cream and the impending pleasure you are about to experience. You open your mouth and lift the ice cream towards your tongue. Suddenly from nowhere, something smashes it out of your hands, you are lifted into the air and struck repeatedly by stinging blows, and your hearing is invaded by loud shouting that distorts the sounds in your head. You are thrown into a pushchair, reeling from this huge experience. You are left reeling and through the fog of shock, the pain in your body begins to intrude – you scream uncontrollably, unable to make sense of this experience. Nobody helps you. You are abandoned – you know now without doubt that you must never want ice cream again. Over time you might, to avoid it, build a moral story to explain why ice cream is bad, evil, and a supporting narrative about how the people who want it are stupid, fat, unhealthy, greedy, or you might experience profound nausea at the thought of it.

You might become a closet ice-cream eater.

You might hoard it secretly.

However you translate this experience into your self-concept, your attraction to and your resistance to the desire for ice cream, either in yourself or in others, will result in it occupying a heightened and anxious significance in your life. Forced to interact in a world where ice cream exists, your Meta-Schematic Belief becomes a guiding principle for all 'acceptable' behaviours relative to ice cream. Ice-cream can pose metaphorically for anything – sexual preference, expressed frustration, need for physical contact/remoteness, territory, peace and quiet, permission, expressed excitement, the need to roar with pain, to become my own person, to be a jazz dancer rather than acquire a PhD in physics, the profound need for contact through intimacy... the list is endless. How else might 'being needy' become a social sin?

Experiences like this teach us poorly constructed lessons about who we are, what our innate, inexplicable desires mean and how dangerous they are to our wellbeing. In adults they lead to multiple emotional and mental distress e.g. PTSD, anxiety disorders, personality distortions, dissociative states, depression. Survival in a dangerous world then requires anxious vigilance – structures of defense, like invisibility, hyper-awareness, contact-avoidance, shyness, being over-pleasing, targeting others for abuse, seductive behaviours, fantasy, numbness, sociopathy, breakdown of one sort or another...the list goes on, start to make sense.

So in summary, each of us learns what we *are* through the types of care or lack of it that we experience in our earliest experiences. If we had a primary carer (be it father or mother) who ignored us when we cried then we learned complex lessons about ourselves, without the aid of reason or insight about the other person(s), from this experience. We learned what others do when we cry. If we had a carer who hit us or shouted at us then we learned about ourselves and especially what we deserved in the future from those experiences.

Being acceptable enough to the world outside to avoid abandonment is vital – not to achieve 'love', but simply to get basic survival needs met. Love as a nourishing condition becomes a remote issue entirely, and one we will explore thoroughly throughout EMSRP.

The Inevitability of a Self, Good or Bad.

A Self is a dynamically inevitable construction. We have to have a self-concept to be able to function in the world at any level at all. Even if my 'self concept' suggests that I am nothing, that I do not actually exist (a fundamental self related belief that we frequently uncover in participants who experienced early neglect and abuse), I have at least with that a guide as to how I must behave in order to do an impression of existence.

The belief is worn like our assumption that gravity will keep us pinned to the ground. In redirecting all of my adaptive resources into the project you might label *"proving that I do exist even though I know I don't"*, the potential self lying latent and unfulfilled far beyond the limits of "I do not exist" ceases to progress, is put away and neglected while a NOT-SELF is crafted and practiced, tested and refined. We refer to this static potential self as the 'Frozen Authentic Self'.

When it becomes frozen, fixed and inflexible it ceases to be dynamic. It is foreclosed. Foreclosure before language is acquired is a severe, ubiquitous and largely invisible social disability, although, like gravity, tends to exist unnoticed as such. It has unfortunately remained poorly understood and when its currently baffling symptomatic energies pop up uninvited into feelings and behavior, they are all too often medicated into numbness, lazily labeled 'mental illnesses' or 'syndromes' or both.

Now we do not deny that there are mental illnesses with neurological bases that are gradually becoming increasingly evident and better understood. However, put any living being in circumstances that deny their subtle needs any satisfaction whatsoever, and they will exhibit ailments. Deny a plant the right soil and it will wilt, become depressed and fail to thrive. Human beings are the only species to persist in their commitment to the wrong soil and medicate themselves to suppress the symptoms that scream for help; indeed we even make it a personal flaw that we are unable to thrive in the wrong soil – this is what the concept of "resilience" legitimises. Our failure to thrive just serves as further proof that our worst internal beliefs about ourselves must be true. *"There really is something wrong with me. Everyone else seems to be doing fine, but nothing works for me I am so flawed."* Every human has the resources already in place to reactivate the development of their Authentic Self, but it is impossible, unsustainable, without the metaphorical soil being supportive to thriving.

Peculiarly, this wisdom is not widely available in forms; a) that are simple to understand; b) whole and entire progressive frameworks for understanding life; c) practically applicable in each unique life and d) enable a person to go through the process of growing up again from scratch including but not limited by the past. The metaphorical 'can' is repeatedly kicked down the road, and the dehumanizing world of work and play that promotes the very conditions for the 'ailment' is promoted with relish.

Knowing what we *are* is essential if we are to construct someone we are not who can appear when the chips are down, the stakes are high and the outside world threatens us with loss.

The shamed Authentic Self continued to be reinforced through the language of childhood as we developed. Many experiences are brought to bear on the formation of this self-concept, this keystone belief that supports the entire structural form that explains to us what and who we are. Many parents, teachers, carers may quite casually inform a child "you *are* naughty", "you *are* bad", "you *are* a waste of space". These statements act to reinforce the self-concept that informs the child how, in effect, they are responsible for threatening their own life. The statement contains the word *"are"*; it does not distinguish the child from their choice. Rare adults make this distinction – *"That choice was unfair"* is different from *"you are selfish"*. You will hear parents and authority figures routinely and casually making denigrating dispositional statements about what children *"are"*. This suggestion leaves the target in no doubt that this must be so, and that their fixed essence is indeed "bad".

Empowering *choice* is different. Choice is the source of agency. Choice allows for flexible experimentation, learning and adjustment based on findings by the experimenter. What you "are" feels immovable, rigid and irrevocably part of the hardware. There is no choice but to exhaustively obscure and disprove it, and when this becomes exhausting, to hide away or periodically to surrender to binge behaviours, to explode without self-restraint. Reinforcing flawed disposition simply hardens the already freezing Authentic Self and further informs the Meta-Schematic Beliefs and the web of subordinate beliefs that in turn govern the construction and management of the "not me".

So while the infant first learns from the moods, expressions, behaviours of the people in their early environment, the central, or Meta-Schematic self concept first formed by reading the effects of its causes, is later repeatedly reinforced through language– *"you are naughty"*, *"nice girls aren't angry"*, *"boys shouldn't cry"*, *"I want never gets"*, *"stop dreaming"*, *"stop acting like a child"*, *"you're showing off"*, *"now you've made Mummy really unhappy"*, *"God sees everything you think"*, *"you are bad"*, *"little monster"*, *God you're a pain"*, *"Stop wingeing, you whiner"*, *"Why are you always....?"*. It is how racism becomes so powerfully shaming, homophobic bullying, name-calling, trash talking, repeated insults, criticism posing as 'caring guidance' – it all tells someone that what they ARE is flawed, and what they *should be* is something else. Guilt is about stuff you do; you can clean that up through different choices. Shame is about what you ARE and what you are feels fixed, a given, and this is embedded by the idea of the original flaw, dare I say it, the pernicious concept of "original sin".

We had to live as if our self-concept was the truth – without a self-concept there would have been no way of predicting what others would do. When the world responds as we expect then we have the illusion of control. When it responds in unexpected ways we no longer recognise ourselves. Knowing that open desire for ice cream is dangerous becomes a predictive tool for survival.

Living in non-acceptance of the frozen authentic self allows us the illusion of control. We know who we are and this dictates what we should expect and do. Nurturing and unconditional acceptance from others becomes therefore an unbearably confusing conundrum, puts us out of control, in an unpredictable world, vulnerable to the pains and punishments of the past. It awakens all of the frozen hungers. It creates the ground for an explosion of unmet needs into uncontrolled expression – and these become overwhelming to the individual and the person providing the acceptance.

Two people offering 'love' to each other, both overwhelmed by their unmet and un-declarable hungers, will inevitably cause each other tremendous grief. The EMSRP facilitator must be able to accept the participant as they are, distinguish and meet their own needs whilst maintaining the boundaries for the participant as they encounter, own and experiment their ways through their own hungers. Failure to do this can only reinforce the Meta-Schematic Belief, reinforce and justify the need to refreeze the Authentic Self, and repeat with greater conviction the cycles of shame and limitation. This is no mean feat and is the reason why supervision is vitally important for ALL licensed and accredited EMSRP practitioners. Nobody is above this requirement.

Human beings categorise everything.

Without categorising objects, people, behaviours, our own selves and the world around us, existence would be entirely unpredictable. It would occur as unending sequences of disconnected phenomena, chaos in the face of which we would be powerless. Categories make it possible to encounter the phenomenal world in bite sized, meaningful and useful chunks, as well as to inter-relate them by seeing how they and we fit together. The brain is a categorising machine, a pattern maker. It starts sorting things into categories from the first weeks of life and by 3-4 months are able to form quite complex categorical hierarchies *(e.g. Quinn and Eimas, 2001; Behl-Chadha, 1996)*. Each of us had to sort ourselves into categories too, even before we could add one and one to make two. We are able to spot patterns from very early in our lives.

The human mind is so brilliant at this that it can connect complex relationships like hygiene with disease control, the sun with photovoltaic panels to generate electricity, the behaviour of a sphere can become a roller ball vacuum cleaner or a deep sea diving pod. The same mind that accomplishes great leaps of genius is also capable of misguided linking a floating woman with witchcraft, all teenagers with violence, homosexuality with flooding (UKIP councilor 2014), stars with the existence of a god. Even the fully developed and healthy brain is unreliable in the conclusions it draws. The infant brain, recording events and experiences, links them causally to the centre of the universe – the egocentric self. It is well documented that children, whose parents divorce, will almost certainly blame themselves for it. An abused child is likely to conclude absolutely at one level or another that they caused it. In the same way a child who is loved and accepted unconditionally is likely to form a *causally* deserving self-concept, a capacious Authentic Self, one where Meta-Schematically they know they are able to create care from who they are, whilst the one who is blamed and berated, or the one consistently nagged and criticised, another forced to perform behaviours that do not flow from them naturally, yet another who is denied the pursuit of the fulfillment of their innate desires, blocked from fulfillment, denied affection, ignored, used/abused, forced to 'unsay' what they really want to say, to lie about their inner experience of themselves, to swallow injustices without protest etc. will certainly fail to thrive. A child, all of us indeed, must have a self-concept to even exist. The self-concept guides all decision making in the process of the developing self.

So in summary, the Authentic Self results in a Meta-Schema, a grand plan, rigorously patterned. Its patterning process has resulted from the Authentic Self's expression – and expression of it has resulted in consequences, many of which have resulted in the putting away, the hiding and suppression of its impulses. It becomes the part that must be hidden at all costs.

Expressive Meta-Schematic Re-Patterning seeks it out and brings it out into expression where it can be seen and fully understood in its shamed form, and creates the conditions for the natural processes of human development to grow it beyond the limitations of the old rules, to fulfill its impulses, to mature itself in the supportive care of its owner, parented through its constant development by a bill of rights for thriving so that each participant can find their confident place in the social world again as a reactivated, dynamic and developing construction. This is where the freely flowing authentic self was destined to express itself, to guide choice, to take forms, to invite relationship, to be supported into thriving, to be wielded ethically in the construction of an environment that mirrors its own complete image and likeness. This is what Abraham Maslow (1943) means about the fundamental need of the human being to Self-Actualise.

The Authentic Self is both the creator and, ultimately in its fullest expression into the world of things, its finest creation. When it is shamed and debased by the Meta-Schematic Belief it remains a shamed secret, created out of the belief's own image and likeness, albeit obliquely. Yet still the frozen, 'unmatured' authentic self has an essence, a uniqueness that given better circumstances would have allowed it to express and through mastery of tools and resources in the environment, to generate forms that reflected its character. Unfettered by toxic shaming, parented well, encouraged, supported, accepted it could *actualize* i.e. find its fullest expression in the world.

Rediscovering essence and tending it into the world of the participant by the participant, by rediscovering its innocence and parenting it appropriately to its thriving, permitting it to expand past the limits of the frozen boundaries of its shamed form, they create the foundation relationship that enables each participant to be created in their own dynamically expanding image and likeness – including the shamed self-concept brought along and integrated in the journey.

One cannot undo history – to be as free with a grounded and balanced freedom, one must include it fully.

When first I set out on my quest for a simple understanding of my own suffering, I spent many years thinking that the broken little boy in my past who I reluctantly carried with me could be healed of his brokenness. Once I realised that his brokenness is a permanent feature of him that must be accommodated in my self-parenting as I move forward into expanding expression of my essence, I can inform myself how best to 'caretake' the parts of me that carry the patterns of the brokenness. He is a broken little boy to this day and I love me for it. Although able and familiar with vastly greater expression in the world than his Meta-Schematic Belief ever permitted, he still panics when we encounter steps into the world that we have not seen before. Every 'first' shakes his confidence and he lets me know.

The greatest act of creativity is the construction of the conditions in which the Authentic Self can thrive and discover its fullness. To achieve this we each have to resume the role of creator – the composer of the life-music, conducted through our choices, in turn utilising all of the many facets, the orchestra of the unique Authentic Self in the playing out of the music.

It strikes me that although not religious myself, we may just be godlike. *"God saw everything that he created and it was good,"* including the limited, frozen authentic self.

45

That creation enabled us to avoid expressing ourselves at such a level that our shamed and shaming early environments failed to abandon us, punish us to death; this is not such a huge leap of imagination. We have seen what happens to some children whose self-expression is maltreated to the extent that they are beaten, starved or otherwise neglected to death. It must be said here that even great parents have left holes in their children. It is human. We learned to parent from our own parenting by parents who in turn learned the art from their own parents before them and so on. EMSRP is not here to beat up parents. It is there to create better, nourishing and love-in-action parents of self and others. It could be described as a revolution starting from the inside and working outwards.

Successful Self-Actualisation is the ultimate objective of Expressive Meta-Schematic Re-Patterning. On the surface this can appear to be a Utopian objective when seen from the 'not-me', but it is in practice the path of least resistance to the expressing and development of the unfrozen Authentic Self.

Everyone has a very negative Meta-schema that was constructed out of failed infantile social experience. It provides an explanatory, albeit misleading concept for social failures. In later life, the feelings through which it communicates are activated whenever social failures occur. It brings with it the unmistakable experience of SHAME.

"Oh shit, I've been found out!"

So to sum up for the final time, shame issues from the belief that there is something unnaturally flawed in the hardware called "me". It is a potent secret, to be hidden from the world and feels catastrophic when it is exposed inadvertently. It is a Meta-Schematic Belief. It is accompanied by the reddening of embarrassment, and paralyzing shame. It is the force that convinces the individual that they should hide away from others, stay under the bed clothes, not attend the party, the club meeting the family gathering, not ask the girl for a dance, the boy for his number, not speak "I love you". It tells the person what they should say, should do, should pretend to be, should lie about, should never reveal and in equal measure dictates what should not be done — it abhors spontaneity and behaving on impulse because it is then that the flaw will be exposed, and this will inevitably lead others to think badly of, humiliate and abandon them. It crushes new experiences and exploration. We are forced to create an acceptable NOT-ME in order to function and avoid abandonment.

The primary task for the NOT-ME is to hide the frozen authentic self. Keeping it hidden exhaustingly and exhaustively drives social behaviour. It denies the validity of actual, important, in fact crucial needs that are necessary for thriving because the authentic self, where all real deficiency needs reside, lies abandoned, ignored, rejected and even reviled. The need for a hug can never be satisfied by eating chocolate, the need to be praised for an achievement can never be satisfied by getting drunk, the need for meaning can never be satisfied by sexual intercourse with multiple partners, the need for a father to say the words *"I am proud of you"* can never be satisfied by becoming CEO of a corporation destined for burn-out when the Authentic Self's dynamic development cries out for a simple life, for example, as an artist.

The Meta-Schematic Blue Print becomes a multi-faceted construction made out of every experience that threatened to make us unacceptable to those upon whom we depended absolutely for our survival...let alone for love. It guided us in constructing the NOT-ME, a person who carried no evidence of the powerful 'badness', the flawed self. It helped us say the *right* things, claim the *right* thoughts, adopt the *right* views, to scowl at funerals and suppress the laughter, and to smile at weddings whilst suppressing anger or bitter disappointment; to pretend that whatever it was that injured us didn't hurt one little bit even though everything in us felt like yelling with pain; to please others first, second and last and to forget what might have pleased us; to accept abuse, to smile on top of anger and to apologise for our manifold fears, deepest sadness, frustrations and tears of despair. It guided us to deny that our angry, violent outbursts were anything but "totally out of character", to buy into the narrative that people will think that our grief is weakness and that we should smile on top of it; it guided us to stay lonely because we deserved no more than to be with people who served themselves at our expense; it kept us in 'safe' jobs that our fathers said we *should* do or settling for any job, the knowledge that our worthlessness denied us access to the jobs we truly desired, drove us onwards studying subjects we hated with a vengeance but that might get us the "good job" that our mothers feared we might not get if we followed our essential drives. It led us to bully and accept bullying from others, to tolerate being used for others needs without our consent, to use others for ours without *their* consent, to duck and dive and bob and weave our ways through our resentments and faint hopes.   It is the source of what John Bradshaw calls our Toxic Shame. As he says, "We are as sick as our secrets" – so exposing the Meta-Schematic Belief is essential to breaking free from its grip.

So in order to begin to discover the potential of the Authentic Self, we must first locate it in its frozen state, we have to look at this sophisticated web of beliefs, rules and principles that drive so much exhausting, self-defeating behaviour designed solely to obscure what we really most fear we are. This Meta-Schematic Belief, the foundation stone of the NOT-ME we have constructed to avoid the consequences of being exposed, must be encountered, fully understood, seen for what it is and its grip loosened before we can hope to go on to reactivate the developmental journey of the Authentic Self. The Meta-Schematic Belief of course does not want to be uncovered – it demands dominance because it is formed out of the need to survive. Therefore, when it is challenged, its guardian voices will tell us that we are doing something life threatening. This, of course, is untrue – but it *is a pseudo-truth* we have always lived through without consciousness. We know it in our being, not in our cognitive awareness. We have, without knowing it, surrendered so many choices to it that it has become the driver of our most frustrating and immovable default habits. Yet for all the evidence of its untruth, the evidence for its validity is that that we have most espoused – *"I know that everyone will leave me, they always do!"* Spot the person who wants to marry in a hurry and ask yourself, what are they afraid will happen if they take their time?

Learning to communicate this background to shame and the Meta-Schematic Belief is essential for the facilitator. Being able to let participants into the secrets and for them to be able to identify with the principles is essential for them to be able to give themselves permission to do the next, and possibly most challenging process of the entire EMSRP programme.

For would-be facilitators, knowing the anatomy of their own shame is the most effective way to learn to communicate about it to another person. Secure self-disclosure is arguably the most important tool in the facilitator's kit.

In our work together, the anatomy of shame and the Meta-Schematic Belief will, must and does form a large part of our early work together in all forms of facilitator training.

Chapter Two

Part one: SURFACING THE META-SCHEMATIC BELIEF

Ask the client to stand up in front of you as if they are on a stage. Acknowledge that they might feel vulnerable and exposed and that this is both normal and an important part of the process.

Ask them to name a few people from their past who they know they would feel really bad to 'fail' in front of.

Ask them to place each of these people around the 'auditorium' by pointing to a spot for them to occupy, and ask them to picture, or sense them there and name them aloud.

Tell them that you will keep them safe, and that they may feel some powerful emotions.

These emotions are the sign that you are getting closer and closer to the gold seam that we are looking for; they are good news.

The emotions are useful and very important (this is one reason why EMSRP can be more of a struggle with people on anti-depressant or beta-blocking medications).

Ask them to imagine something they can imagine they would be really frightened to do, a scary task, in front of an audience. Ask them to name it. (e.g. "Giving a presentation to the board of directors", "Playing the piano", "Singing a love song to a girl I used to fancy").

Once they have named it – remind them they are in the room with a range of people that they have placed there.

Ask them to imagine trying their best at the scary task – really committing to it and it all going wrong. Ask them to describe aloud exactly how it is going wrong *in the present tense* as they imagine it e.g. "I am trying to sing but all that comes out is squeaks."

The following is an actual transcript of a participant at work in an EMSRP group.

Facilitator: *"You are trying your absolute best but it is all going wrong. Imagine that it's really happening right now – you've committed to your best but it's all fallen apart and you're left standing there not knowing what to do next. What's the worst thought that people in the audience are having about you? Say it out loud. What do you most NOT want them to think?"*

Participant: "They think that I am useless."

Facilitator: *"So let's honour that belief even though it is not a total truth about you, there is a part of you that believes absolutely... that they are right. Say the words "I am useless" as if it is totally true about you, say it to all of those people you placed in your audience including me and look at them hearing your words. Own up to it as if it is a confession. "*

Participant: "I am useless, I am useless...I am useless"

Facilitator: *"What feelings are there around 'I am useless'"*

Participant: "Despair, sadness, I feel small and vulnerable."

Facilitator: Making sure that the participant keeps their eyes open and takes in this feedback *"Well done (name) you are one in a million – most people run away from this place but you, you are brave enough to go towards it. Those feelings are evidence that we have hit the gold seam...you are really good at this"*

Facilitator: *"Now, imagine that this is really true – "I am useless" – If they have spotted something absolutely true about you, what does this just go to prove about the substance of you that you have always suspected might be the case? Something even deeper than being useless?"*

Participant: "I don't deserve love"

Facilitator:- *"Brilliant work, brilliant work (name) – this is the part of you that truly believes it owning up now to the powerful belief. The secret is out there now....what feelings are there around that statement 'I don't deserve love'?*

51

Participant: "I feel like I want to run away and hide, I don't want them to look at me...I feel so ashamed. (tears)"

Facilitator: *"Yes, that's right isn't it – you feel like hiding away from sight. Yet there you are still standing there – that's how courageous you are – well done (name)" "This is the place we have been talking about, we are close to or at the foundation belief that holds you back. Look at us here, the ones who are thinking this thought about you, and say that statement "I don't deserve love" as if it is really true about you. Keep your eyes open and watch us hearing you.*

Participant: "I don't deserve love, I don't deserve love, I don't deserve love – I DON'T DESERVE TO BE LOVED (shouting)""

Facilitator: *"What do you notice?"*

Participant:- "I feel really ANGRY and sad, and my anger and sadness" The participant sobs and closes her eyes.

Facilitator: "(Name) *open your eyes, open your eyes and look at me"* (facilitator is smiling approvingly – approval is essential especially in the face of a part of self that has always been treated with disapproval and disgust). *"You feel angry and sad, and that is right isn't it? Angry and sad – of course you feel angry and sad about not deserving love. You believe this absolutely in this part of your mind and now you are admitting it openly – you are exposing a deep secret. WELL DONE, WELL DONE, you are brilliant at this exercise."*

Participant: "It feels a bit of a relief to say it" Group laughs and several people applaud.. "(laughing) but I still want to hide away"

Facilitator: *"Yes, it's a relief, and still it feels shameful – it's a powerful belief, but now we are really looking at it, and we're going to play with it some more before we're finished – is that OK?"*

Participant:- nodding "Yes OK"

Facilitator: *"So, let's just check that we've absolutely reached the bottom line of this schema, this belief, this big belief – the Meta-Schematic Belief."*

Participant: "OK"

Facilitator:- *"Let's imagine that is absolutely the total truth about you – it isn't really – but the belief wants you to believe it is totally true, so let's go with it to find out where it leads us. Imagining it as true, what does this fact that you do not deserve love just go to prove about you that you suspect is true – something even deeper than that?"*

Participant: "Oh shit!"

Facilitator: *"Well done – that...what is that?"*

Participant: "It proves that I am wrong, I am just totally wrong!"

Facilitator: *"Wrong about something or that the substance of you is wrong?"*

Participant: "Yes , that...I am wrongness it is what I am, just wrong, I don't fit or belong here, I am wrong"

Facilitator: *"That is really, really powerful! 'I am wrong'"* *"Admit this as if it's true to the people in room – look at us and just own up to it."*

Participant: tearful now, shaking voice, "I am wrong, I am wrong, I am wrong"

Facilitator:- *"What feelings are there around I am wrong?"*

Participant: "I feel really small, little, tiny and ashamed – I am....am wrong."

Facilitator:- *"That is fantastic work (name) – stay with those feelings. We are going to applaud what you have done... that might feel really odd because you have dared to reach the place in you that feels the least worthy of applause. But you're a pioneer, you have gone where few people dare to go. And there you are standing there, intact. "*

APPLAUSE (if done in a group, the whole group applaud).

Part two: MAPPING META-SCHEMATIC BEHAVIOURS

Facilitator: *"Now write that down in a bubble in the centre of a page. Write "I am Wrong" and leave a lot of space around it. Think of all the things that hiding this 'fact' about yourself has made you do – what does it force you to do in your life to make sure nobody ever sees it?"*

"What other patterns do you can you identify that it drives?"

Here is an example of a real first draft Meta-Schematic Behaviour Map that emerged in a real session.

Other questions that have proved their value over time are:-

- *How does it dictate your style?*
- *How does it force your political views and affiliations?*
- *Who does it make you avoid/gravitate to?*
- *What does it deny you?*
- *What have you committed to never having/achieving/desiring that your MSB tells you that you simply can't have?*
- *How does it dictate you car choice/job choice/ neighbourhood/friendship group?*
- *What does it tell you about being 'ordinary'?*

- *What does it make you want to crush in others?*
- *What kinds of people does it force you to other with?*

Gradually the chains of cause and effect emerge and the participant can begin to see how much of their adaptive energy is consumed in maintaining a smokescreen. Some participants find themselves unable to write anything at first and may need to be facilitated more actively with suggestions. In group work, often the sharing of elements of these maps, coupled with insightful comments from peers, supports others in opening up to Meta-Schematically driven behavioural habits.

Meta-Schematic Self Concepts that most commonly emerge are -

- I DO NOT EXIST – this can emerge out of early situations of being ignored, failed maternal attachment, or may represent a place of comparative safety for participants who have been physically and/or sexually abused.
- I AM CHAOS – this resulted from an upbringing where there was physical, emotional and sexual abuse in early years experienced by the participant, and frequent paternal domestic violence witnessed; environments where there were no rules or inconsistent boundaries may also lead to this organising belief.
- I DO NOT DESERVE MY LIFE – examples of this have come from participants who have lost a sibling at birth (twins, triplets etc) or in early in infancy, died in utero or as a neonate and been revived, or where an early attachment figure has abandoned them or even died. Examples abound from failed maternal bonding e.g. due to maternal mental illness, depression, economic circumstances. Abandonment and subsequent foster care and/or adoption also may underpin this meta-schema.
- I AM EVIL - this has been particularly evident with those raised in religious family circumstances where splitting (rigid division of good and evil) is especially evident

- I AM DISGUSTING – often resulting from being mirrored with distaste and disgust by carers. Participant 'A' was sexually abused by a stranger in the garden of a relative's house. Puzzled by the experience and not knowing what to make of it, 'A' told relatives in the house minutes later. Unable to contain the news the adults attacked 'A' verbally and emotionally reinforcing a pre-existing conviction that the "disgusting" behaviours of others were, in fact, caused by 'A' – somehow they were 'A's.
- I AM A FRAUD,
  - A LIE,
  - A MISTAKE,
  - AN ACCIDENT,
  - A FAKE
- I AM FLAWED
  - THERE IS SOMETHING WRONG WITH ME
  - I AM NOT GOOD ENOUGH
  - I AM NOT WORTHY OF LOVE
  - I AM WORTHLESS
  - I AM A DUD

One very important property of the dominance exerted by this belief is that the entirety of the owner's 'wrongness' means that it must be rejected publicly as representative in any way of the real-self. However the belief issues from the core of self. Spontaneous expression of its responses to the effects of external stimuli has 'caused' unpleasant and even perceptually life-threatening consequences, each of which has presented experiential evidence that its expression is a bad idea and must be stopped or adapted with urgency. This means that the Not-Me *must* source who it has to become through careful interpretation and testing of the outside world. This causes over-identification with the objects and people who most confer acceptability, for example the beautiful 'trophy' partner, the expensive car, the high flying job, the right neighbourhood, status-seeking etc. Loss of any or all of these smokescreens to the most shamed self concept feels like a threat to life itself. Of course it does, because the authentic self is so completely rejected that it automatically triggers resistance to abandonment. How many successful businessmen have hit bankruptcy only to take their lives by suicide? We know that some men who lose their jobs in mid-life can pretend to all of their closest family that they are still working, getting up on time and leaving for work as normal, whilst actually wandering the streets until it is time to come home again.

The Meta-Schematic Behaviour Map reveals just what a powerful and exhausting motivator the flight from shame is. We at EMSRP.org believe that all stressful over-performance may be driven by flight from, and the profound need to socially obscure, this belief.

Now, many people who are motivated towards their 'success' by flight from the shamed self fear that they will cease to be motivated if the Meta-Schematic Belief ceases to hold power over them. They fear there will no longer be anything "to get up for in the morning". This is a legitimate fear if you believe that the shamed self is all that waits for you if you drop the social mask of the Not-Me. The front is exhausting, and exhaustion begins to short circuit the ability to prevent the shamed authentic self from it natural emerging; tired people might get snappy, as indeed might people under sufficient influence of alcohol or recreational drugs may reach the point of saying things they later regret or do things that land them in trouble. What has been resisted invades behaviour and expresses itself with abandon, unmanaged, immature and without consideration for consequence in the moments of invasion. *"That was totally out of character for me!"* is often the claim.

However, the unformed energy of Essence that began expressing through the innocent child was naturally motivated, replenishing its unremitting energy from its source. What we call 'Unformed Originate Energy', or Essence that drives the infant to explore and master is still there. It becomes hijacked into service to survival and avoidance of being 'found out', to the need to conform to the dominion of the environment. Once this is reassigned into the service of a reactivated developing Authentic Self, of which the dysfunctional self-concept is merely a part, motivation feels different. This is an experience that takes some acclimatisation – it is found in flow rather than urgent compulsion. This shift alone is a significant breakthrough to be fully encountered in steps 6 and 7.

The Not-Me provides a temporary haven from the pain of the shamed self. However, from time to time it recklessly expands beyond its immediate limits, and this presents the opportunity for *manic* relief from the absolute limitations of the shamed self-concept emerging from the Meta-Schematic Belief. Resisting invasion by the pent up energies of the frozen authentic self on top of the effort required in controlling behaviours to ensure no social slip ups occur can become intolerably frustrating. Periodically, the authentic energy erupts when the meta-schematic 'parent' fails. The eruption is uncontrolled, clumsy, unsophisticated – there are no parental skills to manage it into the world – and unboundaried, unmonitored and unmanaged authentic expression explodes into the environment. This 'fuck it' and abandoned expression provides a short-lived experience of pseudo-liberation.

It takes little to penetrate the thin and unprotected walls of the manic Not-Me. Any evidence that it has been 'seen through', followed by the inner voices of paranoia and the person is forced back into self-doubt, negative self-talk and withdrawal into shame and stuckness – in fact by degrees they spiral into the misery of depression.

The next two elements of the EMSRP process are essential in the pursuit of liberation from Meta-Schematic constraints. In order to escape from the grip of both the Not-Me and the frozen Meta-Schematic self-concept we have to find another place or places for the participant to occupy and from which to experience themselves. We need to first make powerful choices that defy the rigid rules, compulsions and Meta-Schematised behaviours by committing to novel behaviours, public breaches of the rules as *controlled* acts of wilful defiance. The source of choice to break the cycles of meta-schematized behaviour has to emerge from elsewhere in the psyche, somewhere new, another unfamiliar 'self' must be brought into play. Locating and identifying the belief, the public confession of it and the exploration and mapping of its compulsions are a start. However, the profound shift is enabled when the person who has boldly exposed and explored it, then turns the creative tables on the belief itself. Having been passively created BY the belief, the next step requires a deliberate act of creativity WITH the belief.

The belief instantly becomes a creative resource to be masterfully utilised rather than the tyrannical master to be feared and obeyed without question. We need now to *demonstrate* creative dominion over the Meta-Schematic Belief. The process is best explained in this next series of graphics.

1.

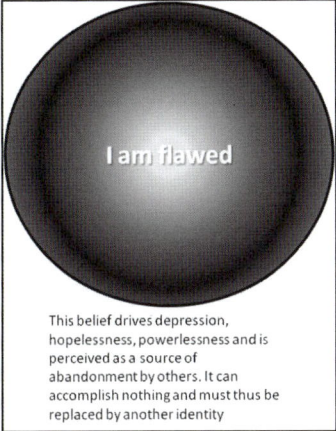

This belief drives depression, hopelessness, powerlessness and is perceived as a source of abandonment by others. It can accomplish nothing and must thus be replaced by another identity

2

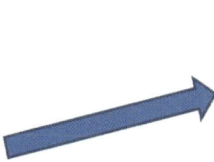

I am flawless

This belief is manic, unsustainable, takes enormous energy and is often reckless. It is the 'seducer' of potential partners, employers, authority figures, gatekeepers to necessary resources. In extreme cases this drives the manic phase of bi-polar depression.

This belief drives depression, hopelessness, powerlessness and is perceived as a source of abandonment by others. It can accomplish nothing and must thus be replaced by another identity

The only escape from the shamed self-concept is another — this demands constructing and committing to the Not – Self, a manic self-concept which is not sourced in flowing originate energy. The energy must be 'manufactured' and thus it is unsustainable.

3

I am flawed

I am flawless

This belief is manic, unsustainable, takes enormous energy and is often reckless. It is the 'seducer' of potential partners, employers, authority figures, gatekeepers to necessary resources. In extreme cases this drives the manic phase of bi-polar depression.

This belief drives depression, hopelessness, powerlessness and is perceived as a source of abandonment by others. It can accomplish nothing and must thus be replaced by another identity

4

I am flawed

You Got It Wrong
I am flawless

This belief is manic, unsustainable, takes enormous energy and is often reckless. It is the 'seducer' of potential partners, employers, authority figures, gatekeepers to necessary resources. In extreme cases this drives the manic phase of bi-polar depression.

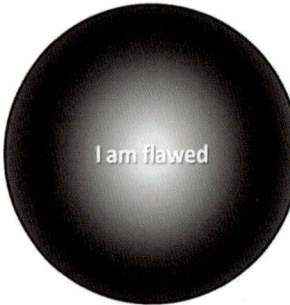

Being back here may be hopeless – but it can be all too familiar.

It only takes a public 'failure', or one person to give the 'wrong' type of look or pick a well aimed critical phrase amounting to "there's something wrong with you isn't there?" and the flawless haven disappears and the victim is whistled back instantly into shame – accompanied by all of the inner voices which reinforce the shame. "Oh shit why did I do that! What an asshole I am" etc etc etc.

It is made bearable only by the creation of justificatory narratives – "I'm just the sort of person who nobody understands", "marriage is not for me" , "nobody should be married", "they're all idiots" – "I hate people with kids" etc

One key way to make this a bearable place is make it special – "I am so flawed I am unique – nobody is as flawed as me and therefore they can never fully understand me. No-one can 'get' me."

5

I am flawed

I am flawless

Going between these two identity 'positions' can be all there is – no hanging around in the mid-zone. It is like being a broken trumpet in the corner of a rehearsal room, never to be played in public, or pretending to be the best and most perfect brass instrument in the world, and totally missing that there is a whole orchestra with which to play. One man put it to me at the end of the programme, "It's like I am this house with multiple floors and hundreds of rooms – and I spent years in the downstairs toiled with the light off thinking that was all there was!"

So how do we experience being more than these two possibilities, waiting for a rescuer, medication, a lucky accident or life after death to deliver us from it?

6

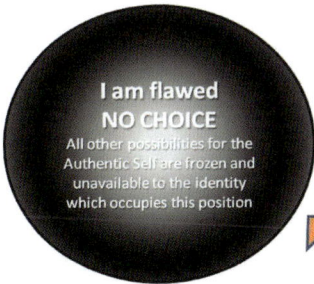

The two personae – the FROZEN AUTHENTIC SELF and the NOT-ME Self are a 'closed' system. There is no other position within it except to escape into invisibility through numbness (a syndrome to be explored later).

I am flawed
NO CHOICE
All other possibilities for the Authentic Self are frozen and unavailable to the identity which occupies this position

I am flawless
NO CHOICE

EMSRP takes the participant to another position outside of this closed system. The Meta-Schematic belief creates a blueprint for behaviour – once the participant makes a choice which is deliberately contradictory to the default behavioural blueprint they demonstrate mindful power to make non-schematic choices as "the CHOOSER". Once this is done, the participant then commits to creative acts using the Meta-Schematic belief as a creative resource

THE CHOOSER

Once this is done, the participant then commits to creative acts using the Meta-Schematic belief as a creative resource, they experience the reality of their CREATOR. Now they have created with the MSB as opposed to being the creation OF it.

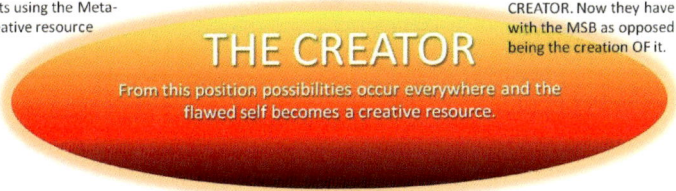

THE CREATOR
From this position possibilities occur everywhere and the flawed self becomes a creative resource.

61

Part three: SETTING HOSTAGES FREE

The Meta-schematic Belief does not allow for truly loving relationships to thrive – it tends to hold partners hostage to its demands. This default behavioural habit is the next in line to be broken and replaced through this next part of the process.

Breakthroughs are sourced in behavioural responses to unreasonable requests. Consider the phrase, *"If you continue to do what you've always done you continue to get what you've always got"*. Change results from doing something you have always NOT done. It is not reasonable to deliberately throw yourself off a platform 200 feet above the hard ground. Reason dictates that you will die as you hit the ground. Wearing a bungee does little to convince the viscera of the uninitiated jumper that they will be snatched from the jaws of death before they hit the ground, but the intellect is convinced enough for it to permit them to do this. It is a breakthrough – a response to an unreasonable request. Jump when everything screams "DON'T MOVE!"

This next part of the process is unreasonable in exactly the ame way. We are going to prove that the Meta-Schematic self-concept does not represent

1) The whole self (i.e. there are other places to experience being oneself in part and in whole).

2) That its guidance is flawed and based on obsolete environmental needs.

3) Self-disclosing secret 'truths' and further defiance of its rules result in degrees of palpable liberation.

Everything the Meta-Schematic Belief insists upon is secrecy therefore we are going to traduce its laws. Secrecy is "reasonable".

In a group each person gets the opportunity to stand in front of the group, one-to-one they stand in front of the facilitator. In both instances they are invited to populate the 'audience' (real or imaginary) with imagined people from their past and present who they particularly fear being 'found out' by.

Each person is given time to picture this situation and imagine themselves about to do something risky in front of them.

Once they feel ready they are given this form of words. Starting with their most shaming M.S. Belief – they state it as if it is an undeniable fact

"I AM (M.S. Belief) –
I AM WILLING FOR YOU TO BELIEVE THAT ALL I AM IS (M.S.Belief) –
I SET YOU FREE TO BELIEVE WHATEVER YOU CHOOSE –
I RESIGN FROM MY PRETENCE-
I SET MYSELF FREE TO BE ALL THAT I AM WITH NOTHING LEFT OUT."

Each person repeats this until they accept it and resign from secrecy. The point is made that allowing others to believe what they want about us leaves both us, and them, free. Convincing people that we are not our Meta-Schematic self means that we can neither love them nor can we possibly receive their love or be fed by it, we can only take them hostage to our lie. We at EMSRP.org do not believe that relationships thrive when someone holds another person hostage. The scripted statement is the first act of setting hostages free, without a ransom, any expectations or demands of any kind at all. As the great actor Sir Anthony Hopkins says, *"What other people think about me is none of my business"*.

Part four: BECOMING THE CREATOR

Having confronted the Meta-Schematic Belief, owned and admitted to its 'truth', explored its drives and compulsions and resigned from all need to smokescreen it from the sight and minds of others, the final step is to assume the mantle of the CREATOR in relationship with it. All associations with the idea of a god as the creator are not intended here,

63

although the Christian deity of the Bible provides a good metaphor. In this respect we may indeed be made in the image and likeness of a divine creator, if there is such a thing. The Meta Schematic Belief creates each of us in its own image and likeness, and demands its behaviours are performed in the name of salvation from past pain.

Participants are briefed to think of a common song tune – a simple melody e.g. *Happy Birthday, I do Like to be Beside the Seaside, She Loves You* by the Beatles – preferably one with a relatively jaunty rhythm. Once they have chosen a melody, they are briefed to write a song to those lyrics with the title being their Meta-Schematic Belief.

This is likely to spark off a bout of Meta-Schematic shame. Those whose belief is *"I am not good enough"* are most likely to start to respond to the task from their prevailing belief – nervously inquiring *"Oh, do you mean write a song? Do we have to perform it?"* The facilitator will need to point this out – to nip the voices in the bud by letting participants know that this is inevitable – of course the voices are going to have a lot to say about this – we are breaking the core rules of the Meta-Schematic Belief.

As an antidote, the facilitator tells them that the song has to be "bad", low-standard, imperfect, rubbish – but it must contain the words that best describe the Meta-Schematic Belief. The song should include some of the behaviours identified on the Meta-Schematic Behaviour Map. Sometimes this is set as an assignment between sessions, and sometimes, especially in group formats, it is done there and then.

We find that shorter periods (5-15 minutes) for creativity are often much better than longer periods (30mins to 3 hours). The song is a simple act of creativity, and they are instructed to have fun. In groups this is particularly powerful. After the period composing they are asked to perform it one-to-one to the facilitator and the room filled with the imaginary crowd used in the first part of the process. In a group setting each person gets to perform individually.

Each person arrives at the front of the audience and uses the following script.

"I AM (M.S. Belief) –

I AM WILLING FOR YOU TO BELIEVE THAT ALL I AM IS (M.S.Belief) –

I SET YOU FREE TO BELIEVE WHATEVER YOU CHOOSE –

I RESIGN FROM MY PRETENCE-

I SET MYSELF FREE TO BE ALL THAT I AM WITH NOTHING LEFT OUT."

They then perform their song with gusto, marking the end of it by saying "Thank you", after which the audience applauds (facilitator, group present, and the participant is asked to watch their imaginary crowd going mad with applause).

The LIVE witnesses are then asked to reflect back to the person who has just performed *"What worked about them when they were performing?"* One-to-one the facilitator gives simple and generous feedback. (Be aware to avoid 'good advice' and veiled criticism posing as generous feedback and guide the audience back to generous and simple feedback about what works about the performer). Check that the participant has heard what has been said to them. For example,

"What did you hear them say?"

"Did you take that in?"

"Don't tell us why it isn't true, just accept that the world sees you in this positive way when you are creative with your meta-schematic and limiting beliefs"

The participant is asked to sit down and to say their Meta-Schematic Belief as if it is true and asked how it feels now.

In almost all cases there is a shift that is marked in their energy – almost always they will reflect that it seems like *"nothing,* now" or *"I can't believe I gave it so much power!"*

To quote a recent participant *"It felt good to get those lines out, they make a meaningful and comforting mantra."* For another, *"I feel like I've taken a blue pill and seen the Matrix."*

If the participant says it still seems powerful then ask them to perform it again and to shout it as loudly as they can whilst making large gestures. The whole group might be invited to sing along, the facilitator might join in.

Part five: HOW THE META-SCHEMATIC BELIEF SERVED US.

Finally they are asked to look at how the Meta-Schematic Belief has served them – what has been good about it?

Give them time as this is likely to be a difficult concept to grasp. The Meta-Schematic Belief associates with powerfully negative feelings and negative outcomes i.e. it has emerged out of failed negotiation with the environment.

Its value was to protect the participant from further damage – if, for example, crying invoked violence from a carer, then suppressing the crying was a valid survival response. To have continued to cry might have induced abandonment or resulted in lethal attack. A more subtle instance would be the child who, having been treated as invisible except when being of use to their 'carers', did well to accept their invisibility and perform usefully in order to survive. The Meta-Schematised behaviours were all designed to achieve survival in circumstances where to have continued in free flow might have served to intensify threatening responses from the outside world of the time.

That time has now gone – but it left in its wake a set of habits based in this core belief, habits that often succeed in recreating the conditions that necessitated the Meta-Schematic behaviours in the first place, a powerful self-fulfilling prophecy. As one person reflected back to me; *"It is like a child who is knocked over by a wave and learns to fear the sea. They grew up and although the wave is tiny to their adult body, in their mind the wave still towers over them and threatens to wipe them out"*.

The Meta-Schematic Belief has done its reasoning and uploaded it into the programming.

The assignment for Step One is to continue mapping the schematic behaviours using the map. They are asked to notice it at work in their lives now they are sensitised to it?

The face-to-face participant is encouraged to email or Skype message their thoughts and insights to the facilitator whenever they feel like it with a guarantee that all will be read. They may or may not warrant a response. In groups, they will be buddied up with one or two partners and will be required to write their insights and findings to each other.

END OF SESSION

Chapter Three

"It's Never Too Late to Have a Happy Childhood"

The aim of Step Three is to begin the process of the participant learning to parent their disowned and unmet inner needs, and to develop a Bill of Rights for thriving that can begin to live in the participant's real world under their active management and control. The rights will be taken into life in stages through assignments carefully designed and scripted to embed them in their social relationships.

The Meta Schema is a 'black and white' belief system and does not entertain shades of grey. If the participant has been convinced that they are worthless, this is not by degrees, it exists as a *total* belief system. They will have introjected (placed inside themselves) the abandonments, messages and punishments that informed its construction.

When authentic feelings and motivations emerge in the form of urges to express behaviours that arise from chronically unmet needs and responses to life itself, they will automatically be 'parented' according to the default plan. This way a world is constructed around all unmet hungers – and any environmental stimuli that contradict the rigid frameworks are molded to fit, ignored, rejected or simply suppressed.

Until this sophisticated system is exposed it continues to cheat the participant of satisfaction of background needs. We must first identify the Meta-Schematised self-parenting patterns; these are so deeply and unconsciously ingrained that asking the participant what they are and expecting an informed reply is a fool's errand.

Part one: F**K UP THE BABY'S FUTURE.

A sheet of flipchart paper is prepared (group work) with the photograph depicted here at the top or in the centre leaving plenty of room beneath or around it. One-to-one this is achieved with the picture, a piece of A4 notepaper and the participant's notebook open and on a clean fresh page.

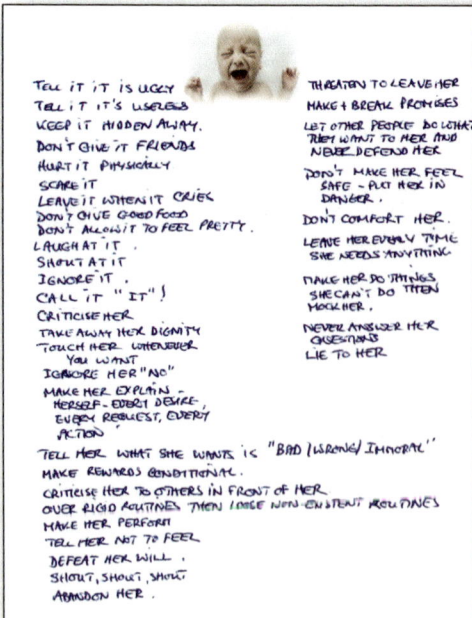

Facilitator: *"Here is a baby. Imagine this baby is given into your care. You are in charge. What could you do to make sure that this baby is well and truly screwed up now and into the future?"*

This request can be met with a spectrum of reactions from anger to dark delight. The request is designed to have impact – and the participant's reaction needs to be acknowledged, made normal and included.

Facilitator: *"Now I know this is an unusual and unexpected request – but what I want you to draw upon is everything that you can think of that would guarantee that this baby turns into a screwed up adult. There is no baby really, it is a picture – let's do our best to write up a list of everything we can think of to really screw it up."*

Write down everything that they suggest under the picture. Most participants have little trouble thinking of things that can be done or denied the child. Sometimes items on the list can induce memories of past abuses – if possible do not linger or divert into processing these memories; draw them back to the present baby in front of them and the list of things that could be done in the future. We are working in the present. The abuses will be dealt with in due course.

This list in the picture above is an example of a real "screw up the baby" list.

When the participant has exhausted their suggestions the facilitator then interrogates the list with them.

Facilitator: *"Wow, look at that list. What impact do you think this will have on the child as it grows up in the world?"*

Let them think about this and respond.

Facilitator: *"Do you think they might have trouble even surviving?"*

Let them think about this and answer.

Facilitator: *"What might their Meta-Schematic Belief be?"*

Let them think about this and answer.

Facilitator: - *"Does she (he) deserve it?"* ask several times to get a 'No' response and then insert

"DO **YOU** DESERVE IT?" to achieve a spontaneous "no" response.

Point out how the Meta-Schematic behavioural blue-print drives these exact responses to inner expressions of need. *"What happens when you have a great idea and you think people might think badly of you if you express it? Find what you do on the list."*

The following list of questions is there as a resource list of fruitful questions that you can explore with clients. This is not a 'must-do' list – asking participants these in quick succession without time to consider responses is likely to leave them overwhelmed, confused and anxious.

- **"How do you do these things to yourself?"**
- **"When your inner feelings try to speak to you what do you do with them that is on the list?"**
- **"When you feel needy, lonely, uncherished, ignored, dismissed, unnoticed – what do you do from your list?"**
- **"When your anger tries to speak its mind to you – which of the things on your list do you do to it?"**
- **"When you have an idea that you want to pursue that is a response to the way things feel at work – what do you do that is on the list?"**
- **"When you are in the face of authority figures and it affects the way you feel – what do you do to yourself from this list?"**
- **"How do you make yourself wrong and what do you do to yourself as a consequence of making yourself so?"**
- **"Ask yourself 'Especially when I am lacking in confidence, which of these things do I do to myself, my creative and spontaneous impulses, and my ideas?'"**
- **"What else can you see in these automatic responses to your needs?"**

Once this negative parenting list has been thoroughly explored and its impact been noted it is time to start the second list.

Part two: WHAT NEEDS DOES THE BABY HAVE TO THRIVE?

Present the same baby in exactly the same way.

Facilitator: *"Here is a baby. Imagine this baby is given into your care. You are in charge. What could you do to make sure that this baby grows up confident, well and can thrive now and in the future?"*

"What kind of environment will your baby need in order to thrive? What influences and experiences must your baby have to thrive and develop well?"

This list is likely to be much slower in production and require some careful facilitation. People often continue to call the baby "it" – I usually draw attention to this and ask if being referred to as "it" will help her/him thrive. Match the client's own gender perception in the choice. The facilitator must challenge vague terms such as RESPECT, LOVE, and SUPPORT. When such words come up ask them to clarify each one – what would RESPECT actually 'look like' in action?

Here is an example list.

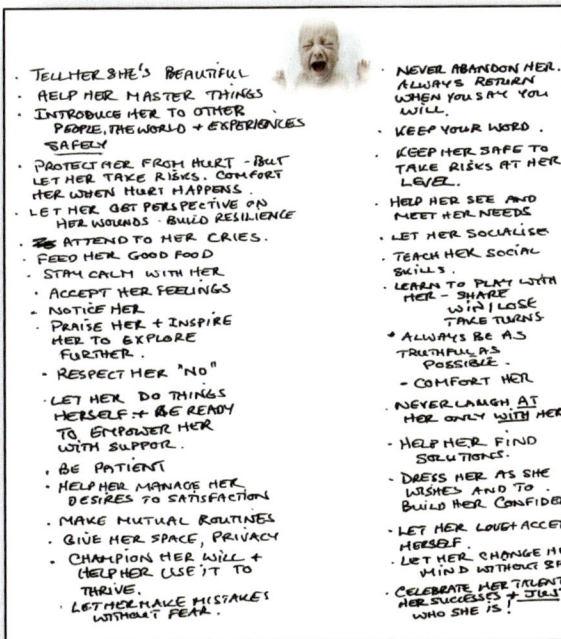

- TELL HER SHE'S BEAUTIFUL
- HELP HER MASTER THINGS
- INTRODUCE HER TO OTHER PEOPLE, THE WORLD + EXPERIENCES SAFELY
- PROTECT HER FROM HURT – BUT LET HER TAKE RISKS. COMFORT HER WHEN HURT HAPPENS.
- LET HER GET PERSPECTIVE ON HER WOUNDS · BUILD RESILIENCE
- ATTEND TO HER CRIES.
- FEED HER GOOD FOOD
- STAY CALM WITH HER
- ACCEPT HER FEELINGS
- NOTICE HER
- PRAISE HER + INSPIRE HER TO EXPLORE FURTHER.
- RESPECT HER "NO"
- LET HER DO THINGS HERSELF + BE READY TO EMPOWER HER WITH SUPPORT.
- BE PATIENT
- HELP HER MANAGE HER DESIRES TO SATISFACTION
- MAKE MUTUAL ROUTINES
- GIVE HER SPACE, PRIVACY
- CHAMPION HER WILL + HELP HER USE IT TO THRIVE.
- LET HER MAKE MISTAKES WITHOUT FEAR.

- NEVER ABANDON HER. ALWAYS RETURN WHEN YOU SAY YOU WILL.
- KEEP YOUR WORD.
- KEEP HER SAFE TO TAKE RISKS AT HER LEVEL.
- HELP HER SEE AND MEET HER NEEDS
- LET HER SOCIALISE
- TEACH HER SOCIAL SKILLS.
- LEARN TO PLAY WITH HER – SHARE WIN I LOSE TAKE TURNS
- ALWAYS BE AS TRUTHFUL AS POSSIBLE.
- COMFORT HER
- NEVER LAUGH AT HER ONLY WITH HER
- HELP HER FIND SOLUTIONS.
- DRESS HER AS SHE WISHES AND TO BUILD HER CONFIDEN
- LET HER LOVE+ ACCEP HERSELF.
- LET HER CHANGE HE MIND WITHOUT SH.
- CELEBRATE HER TALENT HER SUCCESS + JUST WHO SHE IS!

71

The listing process may raise certain issues for example, *"Well I wouldn't want to indulge her too much."*

Facilitator: *"What do you worry might happen if you do?"*

Participant: *"She might become a brat!"*

Facilitator: *"What might happen if everything you did with her was focused on preventing her from becoming a brat?"*

Participant *"What do you mean?"*

Facilitator: *"If you became so worried about the possibility she might become a brat, what might happen to your parenting of her?"*

Participant: *"I might go over the top..."*

Facilitator: *"Which of the two lists might become more dominant?"*

Participant: *"The first list...the one I don't like."*

Facilitator: *"Well, there may be a balance to strike somehow. What might be a well balanced and caring thing to introduce into the second list?"*

Participant: *"To teach here to wait for things, or to earn some of them, to think about her actions and how they might impact on others too."*

Facilitator: *"OK. So there would be room for her and room for other people too?"*

Participant: *"Exactly – I don't want people to hate her because she's selfish."*

Facilitator: *"Well, growing up in a social world is a complicated thing – taking care to fill oneself up, to meet your needs is important but there must be something in it for everyone to achieve balance. This is what we are going to go on to deal with in the next parts of the exercise. But you raise a good point about consideration for others without becoming a total sacrifice to their whims."*

Once the list seems robust then it is time to ask some difficult questions.

Facilitator: *"This list comprises things that your baby girl (boy) will need to thrive. Are there any of these needs-based items on your list that you give yourself? (wait) When you look at this list, can you think of any of your current relationships that offer you any of these things?"*

"So if most of what is on the second list is missing and most of what is on the first list is present, what do you think the impact is on your quality of life?"

> *"After we had looked at constructive and destructive ways of treating a baby it made it easier for me to pinpoint my inner voices and how they were parenting me. It became very clear of how I treated myself in different ways and gave me an opportunity to change the patterns. I also became aware of the relationships I have created in my life that reflect my beliefs of how I should be treated."* **EMSRP Participant**

Part three: CONSTRUCTING A BILL OF RIGHTS.

Nobody was ever born with rights except those rights that someone else was willing to create, declare, stand up for and, above all, **enforce**. To operate in a world with neither a sense of specific rights nor anybody willing to stand up for them on your behalf is to play in the world with no protection. With no protection and no rights anything can happen...AND DOES! The 'anything' that does happen reinforces the Meta-Schematic Belief, and additionally validates the schematized behaviours. Relationships that do not observe any rights, that have no sense of what is acceptable and what is not, that arise out of undeclared need and hidden Meta-Schematic smoke screening behaviours inevitably run on secret agendas that neither party is likely to admit to openly, nor sometimes even privately to themselves. The man who hates women because his mother expected him to act like her absent husband may seduce a partner by pleasing her at every turn. He may wish to marry fast, to reach a milestone that might elude him if he has to sustain his pretense longer than he can summon the energy for. Once married, or with the relationship consummated, the gloss may wear off relatively quickly and the undeveloped and frozen Authentic Self may come steaming out from the dark with all its resentments, unmet hungers and demands in tow. The unmet needs of the hungry child suddenly land at the feet of the partner entirely unannounced. An angry toddler in a three year-old body is there to be supported in maturing his anger; an angry toddler running loose in an adult male body is an entirely different and dangerous prospect. As a toddler he might have had the right to express how angry he felt and for its cause to be traced to his mother's imprisoning agenda for him, for example, that he should fulfill her emptiness. But this would demand a skilled enough adult present to spot and facilitate these needs in both mother and child. Now, once he is an adult, the raging toddler inside him is HIS child to be parented, to be understood and creatively satisfied. On the whole people do not do well in handling these immature emotions that arise inside them as they have never had the opportunity to learn the skills necessary to handle them effectively as they emerge into conscious awareness. Repressed and coiled up tightly inside the frozen authentic self, they can be triggered in a moment, wreaking havoc in all manner of ways.

EMSRP embraces the idea that *"It's never too late to have a happy childhood"* (our thanks to Black, the writer of the book of that name for the title).

A *happy* childhood however requires that the most qualified person to take responsibility for organising the conditions to make it possible is willing to assume the role of excellent parent, to learn the necessary skills and make a commitment to ACTION on the project. The child in the adult runs the show from the default Meta-Schema – that same adult is the person who needs to qualify to run the show on behalf of the wounded child – actually the wounded children, as there will appear more than one as we progress.

Using the two lists the participant is set the task of creating a Bill of Rights for Thriving. The Bill of Rights is for the baby used in the listing exercise. Initially the list can be as long as it takes.

Each right must be expressed as "I HAVE THE RIGHT TO.........." The blank is to be filled in by the participant.

Three rights in one are given to the participant as universal EMSRP rights. Here it is.

"I have the right to say "YES", to say "NO" and to change my mind."

This is set as a homework assignment.

END OF SESSION

*T**he next session*** begins as always with the question *"What is different?"*.

Once this has been mapped and discussed then the focus turns to the Bill of Rights.

The participant is asked to read through their Bill of Rights (usually at this point it is over-extended and there may be a number of duplications. Overleaf is an actual first draft example from a Spanish participant who did EMSRP in English and Spanish over Skype.

Each draft right is explored, and those that are similar are grouped together and distilled. The objective is to achieve a list of 8 to 10 powerful rights. Sometimes there is significant resistance to expressing rights in this format. Some participants try to soften or confuse the message by using other terms. For example one participant insisted on using *"I have the need to feel that I can say no"*. Working through this resistance allowed them to confront their fear of being seen as associated with any single point of view about anything at all. The *"need to feel that I have the right"* left her a victim to the enlightened generosity of others. Her communication was always slow and peppered with caveats and considerations of everyone else. Although

> ### Sample of first draft Bill of Rights from a Male Participant
> ### (Spain over Skype)
>
> - *I have the right to say YES to all my desires and needs, and then change my mind if I want to.*
> - *I have the right to say NO to all the things that move me away from my happiness, needs, and goals.*
> - *I have the right to say NO to all the abuses and injustices.*
> - *I have the right to be treated tenderly, with love and comprehension.*
> - *I have the right to grow up without fear and into a positive and happy environment.*
> - *I have the right to play and have fun.*
> - *I have the right to talk, expressing my thoughts, to be listened and taken into account.*
> - *I have the right to be myself and to be respected and loved the way I am.*
> - *I have the right to have my own feelings (be happy, sad, exalted, frustrated, etc) and express them far away from any shame.*
> - *I have the right to be trusted and to take my own responsibilities.*
> - *I have the right to get success and recognizing.*
> - *I have the right to try, fail, learn from the failure and try over and over again.*
> - *I have the right to have dreams, illusions, set my own goals and go for them.*
> - *I have the right to ask for help and be helped*
> - *I have the right to NOT pay attention to the inside and outside voices that put me down.*
> - *I have the right to choose my job, enjoy it and make as much money as I want.*
> - *I have the right to protect my family, friends and loved people.*
> - *I have the right to be proud of myself, and be happy for what I am and what I do.*
> - *I have the right to think by myself and have my own opinions.*

this had emerged in her meta-schematic blueprint, this was the first expressed evidence of it at work in her quest for parenting. When she saw the pattern she described herself as *"the sacrifice on the altar of everyone else's needs"*.

A right is *an assertion of self-value*, it is a reInforcement of self as an existing object of worth, worthy of defending and nurture, and is something for every adult to claim for themselves rather than to hopefully wait for from others. It is an acknowledgement of normal human vulnerability and the reality that life hurts when there is no possibility for protection. It is a flag to be flown, and above all to be fought for if necessary. Without rights there can be no way to identify and speak about what environmental conditions are negatively affecting the individual's thriving. Emotions are unattached to coherent stories without rights, floating without cogent justification. Unless you have the right to say "NO" whenever it is required, when your anger tells you an injustice is present, you cannot tell people that their demands are bleeding you dry, leaving you spent or otherwise endangering your ability to thrive. Without a right you can never say, "Yes" with assured enthusiasm. Without the right to change your mind, every, "Yes" soon becomes a prison. It could be that the only way to protect yourself then becomes withdrawal from any participation in life at all, or it could become self-sacrificially, even lethally, exhausting.

Striving for these Rights for Thriving in the form of a declaration or assertion commencing, *"I have the RIGHT"* is a vital part of this process especially when it is most uncomfortable to proceed. Resistance can take many forms – if you find yourself becoming frustrated or bored as the facilitator, go back to their Meta-Schematic Belief and you will almost certainly find it at work in obfuscation, muddle, diversion and procrastination.

It may be that a participant is absolutely unable to conceive of herself as someone who could speak these rights, let alone enforce them on their own or anyone else's behalf. This is fine for the moment, and they can be encouraged at this point to imagine someone else, who they can imagine *could* be a mouthpiece for them; this is an inner role model. You can assure them that they will develop skills, write carefully constructed and rehearsed conversations about their rights over the period of the EMSRP process through assignments and practice in sessions. For the present, it is sufficient to write a list of rights for thriving that would, if successfully and consistently enforced, lead to their needs (exposed in the baby process) being met and hungers fed.

Once the list has been finessed and the minimum number achieved, it is important to stress:-

- As the need for new Rights becomes evident, new ones can be created
- As a Right shows up as inadequate it can be rewritten
- All Rights must be afforded to all people in the social sphere in the absence of them having clear rights for themselves – i.e. treat others as if they also have your Bill of Rights.

Rights are nothing if there is nobody to communicate, defend and enforce them. Entering life without rights is to enter it without defense. It means either being ALL OUT there with no protection hoping nothing bad will happen or being ALL INSIDE and shielded where nobody can 'get' you, as illustrated in the following graphics

Option 1.

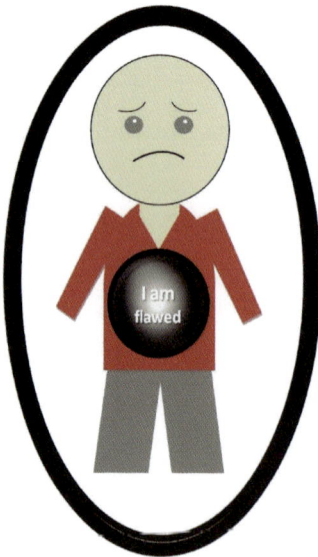

All inside, protected from everyone and everything, but alone - unreachable and unresponsive to life, unable to participate. Unmet hungers!

Option 2.

All outside unprotected, vulnerable – undiscerning about quality of environment, open to abuse – and invasion of shaming paranoia

Option 3

With Dynamic Rights – out and in at the same time – reachable and responsive, able to participate and withdraw approapriately to thriving.

With a Bill of Rights for Thriving, as in Option 3 depicted here, you can be out there in the world, protected by gateways

through which people can approach you, but gates nonetheless you can require people to exit through and to close behind them should you find yourself under threat. Your Rights provide the basis
a) for understanding why you feel threatened, and
b) for a conversation with the source of the threat about why you are taking action on your own behalf.

> *"Numerous times I have acted in a different way and then realised afterwards that I had maintained a right that I had listed in my 'Bill of Rights'. It comes naturally to me now. I have found my voice in situations where I often did not have it and have no problems contradicting people when they try to tell me something is other than it is, when that something involves me."*

> *"The Bill of Rights empowered me as a woman and gave me permission that I had previously believed was not mine to give myself."*

The assignment after this session is to read the entire Bill of Rights to two separate people, not a therapist, but a friend or family member. This is also not designed to 'fix' any relationships – it is purely and simply an exercise in reading the Bill of Rights for Thriving to two human beings.

This assignment is not designed to be challenging out of cruelty, and the instruction not to use a therapist as the audience is to force the participant to locate their 'rights-based' conversations where they will make the biggest difference straight away. For some people this occurs as a shocking request – they have, after all, constructed all of their relationships without the aid of a Bill of Rights for Thriving. Such a conversation is unprecedented and links directly to their previously disowned hungers. It is a vulnerable request. Preparatory time, rehearsal and some script ideas are necessary to make this possible. A conversational script is given, not for them to follow as written, but to open the possibility for a brand new conversation, one that they have never had before, that they can construct themselves.

"I am doing a process to help me with my confidence (or whatever else seems more appropriate) *and as part of it I have to do an assignment that involves creating a Bill of Rights for myself that is designed to help me to thrive and grow. I have to read it to two separate people before my next session. I would really like to read it to you – would you be OK with that? If you don't want to then that's entirely OK and I won't think badly of you at all – you have every right to refuse."*

This conversational script affords the chosen listener with some fundamental rights too – the rights to be *"fully informed before making a choice"* and the right *"to say 'No' without penalty"*.

END OF SESSION

Chapter Four

Becoming the ideal parent – BUILDING INNER TRUST.

*T**he next session*** begins as always with the question *"What is different?"*

Once this has been mapped and discussed then the focus turns to the assignment.

Facilitator: *"What happened when you read your Bill of Rights to.....?"*

When this has been discussed and observations made focus turns to the relationships audit.

Part one: Auditing Relationships

All relationships with others are constructed out of the subtle blueprint of the Meta-Schematic Belief. The belief dictates what is allowed and what is forbidden. This means that all relationships in the participant's life are bound up in undeclared agreements e.g.

"You listen to my unceasing complaints about my life and you do not demand I listen to yours."

"When I want something then I expect you to drop everything to supply it."

"Keep smiling or I don't want to see you."

"You walk all over me and I take it without flinching."

It may be that the participant is the abuser in this dynamic – it flows both ways! This can be a difficult insight to face.

Relationship audit EMSRP

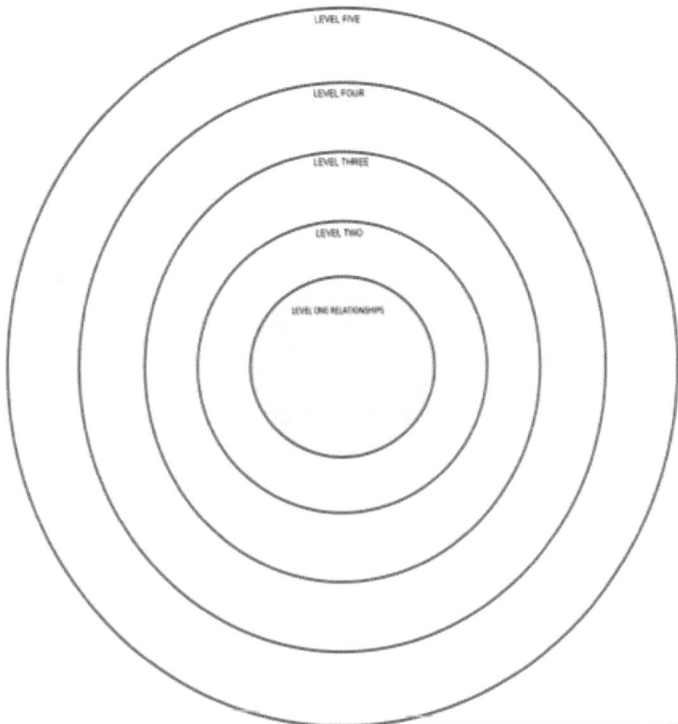

LEVEL FIVE

LEVEL FOUR

LEVEL THREE

LEVEL TWO

LEVEL ONE RELATIONSHIPS

Using a maximum of 5 concentric circles, as illustrated on the previous page, the participant is invited to position actual people in their lives according to their impact on them. They are asked to name them and their relationship to each of them in the appropriate area.

The centre circle is for **level one relationships**. A level one relationship is with a person who has a large emotional impact on the participant. They may be alive or dead, even imaginary people have arrived in the centre circle. One participant had an imaginary lover. As an adolescent this participant had been a social outcast, and this lover became a social lifeboat, evidence that they were loveable in a harsh teenage world of no love and scant acceptance of them. A **Level five** relationship is someone who has little or no emotional impact but is around and about from time to time. The other levels are there as gradations between the two extremes. The participant is given time to talk through each person they select and explore where they think they should be put.

This is not a precise science, and having each person in exactly the 'right' circle is not especially significant.

Be prepared for the participant to want to place you in their chart – you as the facilitator may be already the most loving and accepting person in their lives, or that they may have ever experienced. As the two of you are in a real relationship, albeit firmly 'boundaried', there is no reason to exclude your name from this process, and for them to explore later what rights-based conversation they may need to have with you might be very useful and appropriate.

<u>**Be careful in allowing yourself to be drawn into placing them on your own**</u> should you decide to use one to illustrate people in your life and where you might place them. *"Where would you place me?"* is a red flag question from a participant that, once asked, you must be willing to answer. It might reflect that their unmet needs are attaching to fantasies of what your relationship with them might become. Experienced therapists are likely to be familiar with this situation. If this

is in fact happening then it may be necessary to engage with the facts of their fantasies, to surface what unmet needs are manifesting in hopes outside of the ethical boundaries of the relationship, and for those boundaries to be lovingly restated. The relationship between facilitator and participant is one of love – deep acceptance of one person by the other, which lifts unmet needs even more starkly into awareness. These unmet needs can then be transferred into the hands of the participant as hungers to be addressed through later conversations for thriving in their life.

My favoured initial reply *is, "This exercise is a toolkit to explore the relationships you have in your world and how you have constructed them. Ours is very specifically dedicated to facilitating that process. This relationship is a rehearsal with boundaries. The performance has to be in your life beyond these sessions with the people you want to build relationships you can thrive in. Let's concentrate on your other relationships for the time being."*

Once the sheet is populated, the participant is asked to select someone in Level One and to audit the relationship.

A relationship audit needs to cover the following topics:-

1. Identification of the FUNCTIONS of the relationship *"What is it for?"* and *"What would you like it to be for?"*
2. The current state of play in the relationships in terms of cost and benefit, dive or thrive. (Who is the loser? Who is thriving/diving?)
3. The missing rights from your Bill of Rights for Thriving for you and also for the other party.
4. Identifying and reclaiming the **emotional markers** that inform the participant about **the relationship climate - e.g.** *angry, sad, glad, indifferent, anxious.*
5. What agreements are played out (usually sub-consciously) in order to maintain the status quo.

6. Identify the roles you each play - (e.g. The phenomenally successful son who only gives the good news, the mother who sulks when she gets what she considers 'bad news')

They are asked, *"Which of your Rights are neither present nor observed in your relationship with this person? What is the impact of its absence firstly on you, secondly on them?"* They are asked to be thorough.

During this session they may realise that a right on their Bill of Rights may be insufficiently distinguished or detailed, and a new and more effective form of words becomes available to make the right more robust and relevant – this is fine.

For each Right that is identified as absent ask the question *"If this Right was present and observed in your relationship, how would your relationship be improved a) for you, b) for them?"*

Continue for each Right. Then ask , **"So, what is this relationship actually FOR? What is its purpose?"** This needs to be summed up in a sentence.

E.g. *"It is for him to dump his disappointments in his life at my feet and leave me feeling responsible"* (an appropriate Right for this might be "I have the Right not to be used as a target for anyone's unfinished business with other people".)

"How do you FEEL inside this dynamic? Do you express the feeling or hide it?"

"What roles do you play in the relationship that deliver the status quo over and over again?"

Then ask, *"What would having rights in place make possible for its purpose to become i.e. a purpose for it that you would like?"*

E.g. "It could become a mutually supportive relationship where we both get fed equally".

It may be that the participant realises that they no longer want the relationship, even if it were to change. It may on the other hand be that they have a vision for the relationship that they have never shared with the other person. In some cases their unconscious intentions for the relationship have been positive but different to the other party's, leading to mutual disappointment and frustration. It may be that whatever it may have been for in the past is finished. The question, *"What is this relationship for?"* is powerful and not to be side-stepped. The honest answer provides an insight into reality. Once reality is available, the possibility for creating something new with it becomes available. In any case, each relationship in the audit will require some conversations to be scripted and eventually some will be had with other parties if these new rights for thriving are to be established.

When this has been done ask them to choose **a level two** relationship. Then repeat the same process of auditing the relationship.

Once this is complete, set the assignment.

The assignment after this session is in two parts.

Firstly to continue to populate the relationship audit sheet using the concentric circles.

Secondly, NOT TO HAVE THE CONVERSATION FOR REAL YET. The first step is to write a letter that they are not going to send. The letter can contain

1. **An unreasonable rant if needed – this is permission to let their pen surprise them, to be 'unreasonable' and to vent feelings that may have been repressed for years.**

   Then if possible….

2. **A clear description of the rights that are absent**
3. **How the absence of the rights is impacting on the participant**
4. **An admission of responsibility if possible – e.g. "I realise that I have turned up to this and made it seem as if I was OK with it**
5. **A resignation from the game – e.g. "I want to let you know that I am not going to do that any more"**

6. A statement of vision for the relationship – e.g. "I would really like our relationship to be for us both to ………"
7. If the relationship needs to be over, a statement of letting go and completion without malice.

This assignment is not so much about getting it "right", it is simply about getting it "written". will finesse the letter writing and conversation scripting as we move forward. The elements from 2-7 are designed to draw up resistance and resentments that may be in the way of truly completing the past and being able to have the conversation that could make the difference. If they struggle with them, it is profitable struggle.

END OF SESSION

T he next session begins as always with the question "What is different?"
Once this has been mapped and discussed then the focus turns to the assignment.

The letter is read to the facilitator by the participant as if they are the other person being addressed. The results and learning from the letter(s) are explored.

The most important question to be answered at this point is *"What is the relationship for?"* Another way of putting this is *"What core function does it perform, and for whom?"*, coupled with, *"Does it contribute to your thriving/their thriving?"*

Once these results have been explored it is time to ask the next key question that pertains to each relationship as it has been in the past.

"Given that the relationship was for XXXXXXXXXXXX, what role had you assumed in maintaining that dynamic and what responsibilities were attached to it?"

Sometimes this is already very clear and sometimes it requires some facilitation to surface and define the roles and responsibilities. It can be useful to refer back to the Meta-Schematic Belief at this point and to take time to discuss and reflect on how it is driving these behaviours.

An example is the case of a man who as a child was in the position of protecting his younger siblings (sister and brother) from the anger of his alcoholic father. As an adult this had left him always hyper-vigilant regarding any potential threats to the wellbeing of both of them, even though his father had passed away many years previously. At the age of 48 he still ran himself ragged in service to his sister's and brother's anxieties and with no time or resource left to deal with, or even notice his own. Both of his siblings' default behaviours were to defer all life decisions to him as the older protector. Indeed, the participant had so assumed the role that his conception of his adult siblings was that without him they were helpless and vulnerable to the point of being In constant danger, not just from the world, but from their own incompetence. He clearly resented this and felt burdened by the relationships. Although he could rationally appreciate the capabilities of both of them (both were married and had children of their own as well as being gainfully employed), he could not break free of the 'duty' he felt he owed them. This was having a knock on effect inside his own marriage and relationship with his children, who were treated by him as lower priorities. To cope with this he had himself started to drink heavily.

He had also, as a child, assumed the role of protector and perfect partner to his mother, who had been a victim of physical abuse at the hands of the addicted father. She was aging at the time, but still fit and mobile, but his conception of her too, was that she was in constant danger. So between the three relationships, he had an enormous amount of work to do with nothing coming back in return, as well as demands from his own family unit. All of his energy was harnessed to these relationships and fulfilling his unconsciously agreed commitment.

Once we had answered the questions about his roles and responsibilities, as well as relating them to his Meta-Schematic Belief ("*I am unlovable and deserve nothing*"), he could see just how much of his life was taken up with this situation, understand the mechanisms at work, could see that his siblings were now capable of growing up without him and that his mother needed to be set free from the shackles of his compulsive 'caring and compensation'. The following exercise provided him with such immense relief that he grew physically in stature and sustained this thereafter throughout the process and years beyond it. He could see how much of his limited life-energy was consumed in fulfilling these obsolete obligations for which he had never truly signed a contract to fulfill in the first place.

Put simply, any relationship that does not support thriving leaves three possible options;

1) Have the missing conversations that give it the best chance of transformation into a relationship that does support thriving,

2) Do nothing, tough it out and tolerate the current state

3) Resign from the exhausting roles and re-assign the energy to the creation of new relationships, and/or the transformation of the existing relationship to provide what is needed to the satisfaction of both parties.

Participants are now moving towards a ritualised process of resignation from roles that cost them their thriving. In 'resigning' they get a chance to claw back energy that is then available for them to 'reassign' to the construction of more mutually nurturing relationship roles. Bit by bit they are rehearsing real conversations, arming themselves with repertoires and phrases to empower them when the time comes for a live conversation for rights and thriving in a real relationship.

Resigning from Roles and Setting Self and Others Free to Grow

The participant is now going to write a more finessed **letter of resignation** that outlines

1. A clear description of the rights that are absent
2. How the absence of the rights is impacting on the participant
3. An admission of responsibility if possible – e.g. "I realise that I have turned up to this and made it seem as if I was OK with it
4. A resignation from the game – e.g. "I want to let you know that I am not going to do that any more"
5. Permission for the other party to make their own choices – and to accept that they may not consent or want to change
6. A statement of vision for the relationship – e.g. "I would really like our relationship to be for us both to ...."
7. If the relationship needs to be over, a statement of letting go and completion without malice.

Once written, the participant is asked to read it aloud to the facilitator as if the facilitator is the person being addressed. The letter is then explored through the lens of the Bill of Rights.

Does this letter enforce and support the conditions for their thriving?

How does it enforce and support the thriving of the other party?

It is stressed that this letter may or may not actually be sent to the other party. It might simply empower a change in behaviour within the relationship and inform a conversation that might be essential. The other party is in a relationship with an old conception of the participant and as such needs, indeed has a *right* to be introduced to this new person. The letter is revised to eliminate blame and maximize clarity.

Once the a final draft of the letter is written, the question is then asked *"What vision do you have for this relationship in terms of its purpose and your mutual roles within it?"* In other words, *"How would you like this relationship to be?"* Check that this is clear and it permits the other party to refuse to participate if this vision is not attractive to them. This part of the letter is actually an invitation to the other party to participate in the relationship as a *mutual endeavour* that, although inviting, additionally gives them the opportunity to refuse without penalty.

Once this is done for one relationship the assignment is set.

ASSIGNMENT

"1. Continue your audit of relationships in writing.

2. Sculpt your resignation letter into a form that says what is necessary for you to feel free of old roles and responsibilities.

3. Provide a vision for the relationship that would enable you both to thrive.

4. Offer the chance to say "no".

This is an actual participant's resignation letter to his mother - it is a perfect example of a non-blaming acknowledgement of a relationship within which he was failing to thrive and felt obliged to maintain the status quo out of duty, habit and shame.

"Dear xxxxxxxx,

I have just realised that I owe you an apology. For all of our relationship I have allowed myself to see you with somebody who could not cope on her own, somebody who needed me in order to survive. I know for certain that life is been very difficult in so many ways for you, but you are more than just fragile survivor, you are one of the most courageous and strong people I have ever met. Seeing you as fragile has left me always feeling afraid to say, "no", to you, agreeing to things that I really wanted to refuse-for example, I really did not want to come with you to your mothers 50th birthday. I felt like a spare part and found myself in the middle of your arguments, embarrassed, and wanting to be anywhere other than there. I know absolutely that she would never want me to feel that way. I am in no way blaming you at all for this. I put myself in that situation.

I also notice that I do not share myself with you in the same way you show yourself with me. I assume that you would not want to hear about my inner vulnerabilities, my painful past, my "stuff". I noticed recently that I have begun to resent this pattern, and had a little voice in the back of my mind saying, "Well, what about me then?" Again, there is no blame here-I am the one who has allowed myself to refrain from revealing myself to you. The resentments are not my main feelings towards you, and, I have created a situation that causes them, not you.

So I am writing this to let you know that I do not thrive when I behave like this. I find it exhausts me and stops me from seeing you as the strong, hold human being you actually are. So I am sorry for this. I am going to stop seeing you this way and I'm going to change my behaviour starting from today.

I am going to make myself be truthful with you, not to hurt you, but to make sure that I thrive with you. I will say "no" when I don't want to agree to something so you can make other arrangements if you need to. When I say "yes" you will know that I truly do agree to do whatever it is you invite me to do. I also invite you to be yourself with me. In seeing you as strong it means I can let myself lean on you too. That way we will have a mutually supportive relationship, and not one where I make myself the strong one all the time.

I really want this relationship to be deep benefits for both of us. I want you to know that I love you and that I want the best for you, but not at the cost of the best for me too. So let me know what you think about this. I realise it might seem as though I am criticising you, but I'm not. I take full responsibility for allowing myself to drift into a role where I leave myself feeling short-changed. I want to rebalance things. If you want that too and can see benefiting us both, then please call me or write a reply when you feel ready.

Love,

XXXXXXXXX"

It can be that the vision for the relationship is that it is over and really needs to be discontinued. This is a good outcome too. Our energy is limited, and all of it is already consumed in old roles and responsibilities we never consciously signed up for. We have to resign to make space for something new to be constructed. To resign really means to RE-ASSIGN that energy to fulfilling a bigger Authentic Self. In order to re-assign it, you have to be willing to claim it back.

It is important to point out to participants that the Meta-Schematic Belief and its inner guardians will have a lot to say about this – they will shame them (*"Who are YOU to think that you can withdraw from, abandon, be so selfish etc. etc. etc."*, or most commonly, *"It wasn't really **that** bad."*) This is normal, and a sign that the Meta-Schematic Blueprint is being overridden, and that is what we want. Power is being taken back; the Authentic Self is already being re-parented and thus with no extra effort required, it is being successfully re-patterned.

It will protest.

END OF SESSION

93

The next session begins as always with the question "What is different?"

Once this has been mapped and discussed then the focus turns to the assignment.

The relationship audit should by now be quite advanced, and although it might seem like a laborious task, to the participant it is new thinking. All sorts of dynamics are revealed as they work their way through their relationships. Each relationship will contain impacts resulting from the legacy of absence of rights – the presence of a Bill of Rights for Thriving will now begin to allow the participant to make sense of feelings they have been resisting for some time.

As they realise

a) that the relationship embodies dynamics that contribute to diving NOT thriving (excuse us this one – it rhymes and becomes a useful axiom),

b) the dynamics can be causally defined by finding the Right that is being contravened,

c) the need for a conversation becomes evident and its absence simply prolongs the dynamic's hold over the situation, and

d) the conversation makes space for the participant to begin to reclaim their emotions, **especially anger**, as functioning measures of cost-benefit dichotomies at play. A person who constantly makes demands and makes no contribution is like to make you feel angry.

If your Meta-Schematic Belief abhors your anger then you will have schematised behavioural rules about it, because it was outlawed in early life, and/or you had a Father/Mother who was prone to violent rages or loud and threatening explosive expressions of anger, or indeed you were told that your anger was not valid (laughing at small children when they are angry is common in Sweden for example – and adults tend to laugh when they feel or express anger or witness it in others).

Without anger you cannot read your environment for its costs or benefits to your wellbeing. Anger is almost always an indication that you are present to an injustice. This 'injustice' does not relate to the law of the land, but an innate sense of implied threat to thriving in a situation. Anger identifies a threat to your rights before your conscious cognition gets there. It is "information from within" that calls your intellect and perception into action in exploring what may or may not be present and what you might do about it.

Many of us have learned that anger and punishment are the same things. Many expressive personal development programmes unwittingly encourage and reinforce this point of view. The acclaimed Mastery of Self Expression programme focuses on creative, emotional self-expression; however it coaches people to rage outwardly and to allow their bodies to "express" the anger. What I saw in a decade and a half of facilitating this programme was people contacting their anger, yes, but then exploding into violent stamping, punching the air, verbal threats and insulting expletives at imagined people from their past or present. They hurt their voices, strained and exhausted their bodies and inadvertently bruised themselves from their own blows. I saw anger translated into spontaneous demonstrations of violence and punishment. Whilst the exhaustion that ensues can feel like catharsis, I became convinced that it entrenched the relationship between anger and punishment, and indeed violence, rather than the cultivation of a *creative* relationship with its force.

Violence is a choice as indeed is punishment. Anger, I am convinced, is an invitation to explore its cause in the environment that conscious perception has not yet spotted. It never fails if it is welcomed as a signpost towards deeper inquiry. What Mastery participants are doing is expressing their violence and desire to punish, not actually anger. Anger is information from within. What decisions are made, either consciously or by default, are generally driven by the Meta-Schematic Belief-related blue print behaviours. Participants in EMSRP all notice that once the conversational script emerges that fully expresses the needs embodied in the anger, the emotion subsides, its job done. Anger requires action, of course. It might require violence in extreme situations. But, if the only Meta-Schematised Behaviours are violence and/or punishment, it remains a very blunt instrument indeed.

The Psychologists Oatley and Johnson-Laird (1987) offer the theory that emotions mark our responses to events that impact on goals that have priority in our lives. If our prevailing goal has been hijacked into being a NOT-ME then our emotions will be tied up almost entirely on the success or failure of our watchful vigilance and the impenetrability of a faultless smoke screen. Any failure in the smokescreen real or imagined will result in invasion of emotional markers, subsequent retreat and shame.

The framework below reflects how Oatley and Johnson-Laird divide up emotions – considering how many respected theories of emotion exist from a variety of psychological perspectives, Oatley and Johnson-Lairds' Theory provides the most useful framework for understanding EMSRP and the role of emotions in the process, not just EMSRP but in life itself.

EMOTION	CHANGE IN LIFE PLAN	BEHAVIOUR/ RESPONSE
HAPPINESS	Sub-goals achieved or progressing effectively	Continue with plan modifying as necessary
SADNESS	Failure of major plan or loss of active goal or someone key to it	Do nothing / grieve / search for a new plan
ANXIETY	Self-preservation goal threatened	Stop, attend vigilantly to environment and/or escape
ANGER	Active plan frustrated	Try harder, and/or aggress
DISGUST	'Taste-related' goal frustrated (food, social, affective)	Reject offending substance, people or object and/or withdraw

Commonly in English Culture, women are not allowed to express anger, and tend to have been instructed to suppress It as children. When anger overwhelms their repressive mechanisms they frequently become frightened of it and they commonly (not always) revert to the emotion that in the past would at least express distress, but would usefully minimise the chances of punishment – PSEUDO-SADNESS. Many women find themselves unable to admit their anger, claiming that they need "anger management" or are afraid to be seen as "aggressive" or "hysterical". These descriptions are commonly used in Western cultures to invalidate the emotion in women – and they are learned from the environment.

Men often refer to angry women as 'aggressive', rather than listening to what message lies behind the anger.

Men, on the other hand, tend to have had sadness disallowed as children. The famed cliché "big boys don't cry" is reinforced through many subtle influences throughout childhood in Western culture. They are also not allowed to be afraid. Scared and sad men tend to revert to demonstrations of another emotion that is likely to have incurred fewer penalties – ANGER. In a society that holds anger and punishment to be one and the same thing, this is a dangerous situation. No surprise that women are scared of men's anger, and men fear it in themselves. It is the precursor to male violence. This is a vicious cycle when anxiety about the anger stokes it up.

Emotions, then, contain energy and require at least as much energy to repress them if they are to be hidden as evidence of the Meta-Schematic flaw. Using your own energy to repress your own energy is self-defeating – twice the energy expended in getting absolutely nowhere new.

Each of us has a 'Thrivometer', and its indicators are emotions. All emotions are good emotions because they contain information about our wellbeing in our environment, and in the course of our life-journey.

The 'Thrivomenter' is essential for gauging the quality of our relationships. This step has been dedicated to getting into the nitty-gritty of key relationships. Within this session there are a number of layers to be addressed:-

1) Identification of the FUNCTIONS of each relationship *"What is it for?"* and *"What would you like it to be for?"*
2) The current state of play in relationships in terms of cost and benefit, dive or thrive. *"Who gains, who loses?"*
3) The missing Rights for the participant and also the other party.
4) Identifying and reclaiming the **emotional markers** that inform the participant about **the relationship climate**.
5) Identifying the themes in the relationships that keep recurring and cost most.
6) Roles that require resignation from.
7) Identifying and creating the conversation they are willing to have with a key person that afford the best chance of changing the dynamic for the better.
8) Rehearsing the conversational script.

Now it is time to have a conversation with one of the relationships that has been audited. The participant is asked to choose someone specific to have an actual with them about the absence of a) **the right/rights that is missing** and b) **the impact of this on the participant's wellbeing**. Help them to develop a script to introduce the conversation that invited the other person to the conversation itself.

For example *"I want to have a difficult conversation with you that I have been avoiding for a while now and I wonder if that would be alright. If you don't want to that is fine, but I need to talk this through with you and you are important to me. Are you up for this?"* If the answer is ,"Yes" then the segue into the actual conversation can be something like the following.

"You have a perfect right to be the person you are and to do the things you do. Nobody can take that away. I just notice that when we get together I listen to you and give advice – I have been glad to do that and am happy to help where I can. What I have noticed recently is that when I talk about myself I am left with the Impression that you

feel impatient and close down the conversation. What that leaves me with is a feeling of being unwanted and that our relationship is unequal. I know you'd never want me to feel that way deliberately, but I would love to be able to talk freely to you about my problems too." NOT, **"I've realised what a selfish cow you are and all you do is moan, moan, moan and I'm supposed to listen to your shit with nothing in it for me!"** the latter being what might emerge from bottling up the resentment, but that the Meta-Schema has outlawed.

It might be that the participant discovers that their target person is indeed dedicated to using them for their needs without giving anything in return, and that they are unwilling to change anything about the relationship dynamic. At that point they are left with a choice – do they continue to surrender themselves into relationship conditions that damage their thriving or do they complete the relationship and leave?

It is important to stress to participants that **they are changing the existing relationship agreement** and that in so doing they are breaking the old one. The old agreement was based on their unspoken and unconscious consent to the previous terms of the relationship even if neither of them had ever stated what those were – simply by turning up and participating they consented to and reinforced it.

The other person has not been party to their process of change and their desire to alter the terms of engagement. While the participant will be operating against their Meta-Schematic Blueprint for relationships, the other party is likely to remain unconsciously operating through their own meta-schematised expectations.

Affording the other party some Rights for Thriving too means that they are entitled to be introduced to the new person and their new terms, i.e. the participant's rights that are designed for their thriving and that are on their Bill of Rights are given to the other party by default. They also deserve the opportunity to feel the impact of being treated with the same rights, which can be a new and beneficial experience. Often this can and does have most surprising transformative impacts on relationships, ones that at first view may seem completely beyond repair.

Boundaries beget boundaries, and often the participant's new behaviours act as a subtle role modeling influence on the other party.

The first assignment after this session is to have a conversation for Rights with two people who are level two in the concentric circles or beyond – not level one yet. The second concurrent assignment is to continue with the relationship audit using the questions "What rights are absent, what rights are present and what is this relationship for?"

Setting this assignment can often feel problematic to therapists and counselors as it involves being more directive than the therapist's art normally requires. Participants will feel challenged, nervous and unsure about this – and to prove to themselves that they can parent their relationships without blame, that they can stand for and declare their rights inside real relationships without blame is a core breakthrough for EMSRP. Good parenting requires the ability to have difficult conversations when a child's thriving is at stake. The participant's thriving is at stake. Participants rarely have difficulty with this assignment; but therapists often imagine they will and thus feel almost apologetic to be asking them to do this essential assignment. Communicating rights is at the heart of wellbeing – without the ability to do this the person is condemned to accepting what they get handed, i.e. becoming a victim, or avoiding contact at all.

<u>**ASSIGNMENT:**</u> *"Have a conversation with a key person designed to:-*

1) Introduce the new you to them,

2) Inform them of a dynamic that has been impacting negatively on you,

3) Let them know about the right you have given yourself in order for you to thrive, and

4) Offer them an invitation to play differently in the relationship.

5) Create no blame – they have the right to continue to behave as they wish just as you have the right to let them know that you will not provide that permission any longer. In this case they will have to find the service elsewhere as you no longer consent to it."

END OF SESSION

The next session begins as always with the question "What is different?"

Once this has been mapped and discussed then the focus turns to the assignment.

Each participant will be rich with feedback about the results of their conversations. While it is rare for them to have abject failures, facilitators will have to be prepared to help participants separate the wood from the trees in the cases where other parties have abreacted. Sometimes what at prima facie resembles a disaster is often a major breakthrough. Any new response from the other party indicates a shift in the relationship dynamic.

A woman bullied to the point of near suicide by a controlling and abusive husband calmly announced that she wanted to let him know that she was no longer consenting to be a focus for his abusive outbursts of temper. She assured him that this was a rule for everyone around her, and not him alone. She told him, *"What you need to know about me is that I am determined to thrive in my life and will no longer accept any behaviour that threatens that."* She informed him that she would withdraw permanently from any relationship with anyone who was committed to threatening her wellbeing in any way at all.

He looked stunned and left the room. He came back later and cried in an effort to gain her sympathy (an infantile Meta-Schematic strategy), which she refused to give as her emotions told her she was being manipulated, although his behaviour was unprecedented and surprising to her. She felt powerful for the first time in her relationship with him. Although this was by no means the end of the issues and finding his strategy had not worked, he then apologised for his years of emotional abuse. This was also entirely new. He then tried to force her into *"loving him again"*, and against that potential threat she defended herself using two rights on her Bill of Rights – *"I have the right to say 'No'"* and, "*I have the right to make my choices freely and without coercion from other people"*.

He stormed out into the night leaving her feeling very powerful and quite amazed by the woman she had found herself able to be. Although there were many occasions later that he tried repeatedly to manipulate her further, and she detected each attempt as it happened and thwarted it with her rights, this was the first breakthrough step for her in constructing a new life. She is now in a new relationship in that she is treasured and growing. Her abusive husband has not experienced his own breakthroughs yet – and of course that is his choice. She is free from the abuse; he is free from the situation in which his abuse was doing damage. I genuinely wish him well for his future – he would be substantially aided by an intervention such as EMSRP.

A **right** specifies the terms for someone's engagement with others, goals for dynamic behaviours that serve the vision of thriving inside a relationship that is purposefully **'for'** something. Once a meaningful right is in place it immediately becomes linked to emotional markers that measure its effectiveness. Before children under 10 years of age were finally freed in 1878 from the lethal factories of the 19th century, they had been the targets of a series of legislative steps that gave them rights. The presence of these rights enabled to public to speak about their discomfort at seeing children working long hours in terrible conditions. Prior to the rights being in place, the conversational scripts to champion the rights and safety of children did not exist, and the 'useful child' was commonplace. A right provides a context to explain and speak about feelings that mark psychological impacts that would otherwise be ignored, mis-communicated, belittled by comparison to others who, *"Just get on with it – what makes you so special?"*. Rights enable participants to be happy to be angry, to be happy to be sad, to be happy to be disgusted, to be happy to be euphoric, *and* to be happy to be anxious and use those emotions exactly as they are to guide them in what action to take, with whom and in what domains of their life. The feeling as it is becomes instantaneously useful, and does not need to be altered simply because it is labeled 'unpleasant'. It is a guide.

Happiness in EMSRP is NOT an emotional state; it is a state of acceptance – of self and all of the inner tools and phenomena that exist for the self's successful growth and burgeoning expression into the forms that express it in the world around us. I am happy to be depressed these days – it calls my attention to needs I am ignoring, and permits me to create the space and permission I need to care-take myself. I am happy to be angry; anger calls my attention to things that are occurring in my environment that without rights would impact negatively upon my thriving. I am happy to be sad, it reinforces those relationships I treasure, the activities and objects that are most meaningful and reminds me of my capacity to attach deeply and to love. Happy is not juiced up euphoria, nor is it mania that says "fuck it, and fuck the consequences."

So this session is most likely to see participants returning surprised and energised by their experiences of standing up for their rights, within relationships that have hitherto not reflected, respected or embodied any at all. They may be frightened and baffled by their power, or heady with it to the point where they have tried to bite off more than they are yet skilled enough to chew in other relationships. It is also important to slow down the reckless and identify any sign of brakes-off mania enforcing itself.

Participants deserve celebration for their courage, their newfound power and their determination to live better – and praise by the facilitator is pivotal at this point. Without praise they will fall prey to their inner voices of shame. Newly reclaimed power almost inevitably comes with its aftermath – like vertigo to the person who climbs too high for the first time – it takes the forms of shame. The Meta-Schematic Belief and its guardians are likely to kick in with their points of view as to how and why it is dangerous to have rights. *"I might become the bully if I keep listening to my anger".* This is why the Rights must always be afforded to others – those who almost certainly have no rights distinguished for their own rights to Thrive. Thus to be assured that we as participants remain ETHICAL, we need to consider what it means for them to have each of our own rights. As with exercise, it is important to increase at a safe and steady rate to minimise the chance of injury.

Part three: Making right my relationships in that I have been the abuser

Now it is time to return the favour. The process now is the auditing for the participant's abuses in relationships' with others. *"Where have you not been affording rights to others?"*

"That specific rights have you been denying them (bearing in mind you did not know that you or they could have rights at all)?"

"What have you been using the relationship for without the full knowledge and consent of the other person?"

"What have been the impacts on the other person?"

"What is the missing conversation that will set them free from this dynamic and let them know how they can expect to be treated in future?"

Assignment

"Between now and the next session have two conversations to repair the past without expecting any reciprocation at all. One where you acknowledge your abuse of the other person."

END OF SESSION

Chapter Five

Reclaiming the wounded children.

*T**he next session*** begins as always with the question "What is different?"

Once this has been mapped and discussed then the focus turns to the assignment.

This process ensures that the participant is able to encounter an early experience within which they had no rights and had nobody to stand up for them in any way. This is a formative experience that informed and reinforced the Meta-Schematic Belief as well as reinforcing its behavioural blue-print.

In reliving the situation as an adult parent-to-be they can assess the needs of the vicitmised child and thus have a context for the parenting assignment they are about to embark upon. This 'wounded' child will become the focus of a later exercise – but for now we will find him/her in the height of an emotionally charged experience and assess the circumstances and needs of the child. In the life assignment set up at the end of this session, the child will be represented by an ordinary egg – raw, fresh and with an intact shell. The participant will be instructed to take this egg everywhere with them for two weeks and to ensure its safety in all environments. The objectives are – 1) TO ENSURE IT IS SAFE FROM DAMAGE, 2) TO MAKE SURE THAT IT IS UNDERSTOOD IN ALL ENVIRONMENTS and 3) THAT IT IS NOT LEFT, ABANDONED OR PUT AT

RISK THROUGH ABSENCE. Exploring the patterns of care has proved to be extremely insightful for participants.

Encountering the Personified Meta-Schematic Wound.

Facilitator: *"I am going to invite you to come with me on a visit to a part of your mind where you hold some memories about your life. I am going to accompany you, the adult parent in training, to support you as you visit an early version of you, who found him/herself where there were no rights, no protectors, no defenders to shield you from the force of events. We are going to have a look at the situation and I am going to ask you to describe it to me in the present tense –e.g. "I am standing in a room – the room is warm/cold etc". We are going to look together to see what is happening and to assess what needs to be done for the little person to be set free from what he/she learned about him/herself, and the rules he/she made up from it. So, as someone who has a Bill of Rights for Thriving you can ask yourself which rights would be most valuable to him/her if there had been a good parent involved."*

"To get there we will do a relaxed closed-eyes exercise where we will imagine that we fly up out of our bodies (and up into the clouds and then we will float down to another place and time that will appear to originate in your past and that will play out like a video film or dvd – we will be able to fast forward, freeze frame or rewind it as we wish."

The process starts with a relaxation session – with the participant in a comfortable position, sitting in a chair or lying down. Most therapists or counselors will have their favoured processes for relaxing participants, and for this it is important to remember that the result is more important than the method chosen for inducing it. This is presented as one that we might use, but it is not presented as the best.

We use an ascending visualization process. First the participant is helped in achieving a comfortable and sustainable physical position. They are then taken through their body parts and invited to relax. We then turn attention to the outside world beyond the room through listening and using any sounds as relaxants. Then their attention is brought within the room – they are asked to notice sounds and to allow them to relax them further. They are asked to notice the air temperature as it contacts their exposed skin; to notice the places on their body where the clothes are in contact. The weight of their feet, legs, arms, hands. We then ask them to engage with their breathing – to notice how it warms their nostrils on the way out and cools them on the way in, and that breathing will take care of itself. They are then asked to notice their inner world – the sounds inside them, the thoughts and feelings, and to let them pass by. We then take them on a journey out of their bodies thought the top of their heads and up into the clouds where they are asked to imagine they can lie on a soft and secure cloud. Once there we count them down to a deep sleep. From the cloud we regress them through their adult life back to a time in their first decade of life, where they were in a situation in that there were no rights, and that the situation was having an unpleasant impact on them. Once this is located and imagined, the participant is invited to communicate having located it by lifting a specific finger, they leave the body they have rested on the cloud and float down to the place and time of the located event where they witness it.

During this encounter the participant is positioned at a distance from the event and the facilitator assures them that they are not alone, that the facilitator is with them and will not leave. The participant is asked to describe the environment in terms of the objects present – then they are asked who is there. Once they have established the other people present, they are asked to describe what they can see happening.

Once they have responded to this, they are asked to read the expressions and moods of the people involved – how is each of them feeling? Now attention needs to be placed on the victim of the scene –

"What are they feeling?"
"What are they thinking?"
"What belief about their self has been formed already?"

"What do they need to know about this situation that would give them some relief from believing they are responsible for it?"

"What would a good parent do in this circumstance to put it right?"

"If a good parent was present in this scene, what would they do?"

"What would the little person here learn from that if it were available?"

If the participant is clear about what is needed then take them through a process where they do what is necessary on behalf of the child.

They will have to

1) Get the child's attention and explain who they are, and to tell them that they are here to deal with this situation – it is important to approach without frightening them further, to be appropriately gentle and respectful etc.

2) Tell them that the situation is not their fault and that the help they have needed for so long has arrived.

3) Ask them what they need in order to feel safe

4) Let them see what a skilled adult does to put such situations right.

5) To speak to the protagonists about what they are doing that is wrong, why it is wrong, what rights it contravenes, and then demonstrate the absolute control of the adult participant to neutralise all threats.

6) If possible to make a commitment to the on-going protection of the child and a promise to never leave them

7) When ready place the child in their own heart by lifting them up in a physical gesture and placing them into their body.

Once the child is inside the body of the participant the facilitator needs to ask the following:

"What do you see on his/her face?" – we are looking for a shame free, distress free and guilt free response that embodies 'relief', 'smile', 'sleeping', 'innocent'.

If, on the other hand, at the point of the questions

"What belief about their self has been formed already?"

"What do they need to know that they cannot know from this situation?"

"What would a good parent do in this circumstance to put it right?"

the participant is confused or unable to distinguish what is needed despite being reminded that they have a Bill of Rights for Thriving that they hold on behalf of this child, then gently and patiently tell them to offer to take the child by the hand and explain who they are. They are the big, grown up version of them and they are there to learn how to put things right for them. Tell them that they are going to take them away from this situation and put them somewhere much safer until they have learned the skills necessary to come back for them. Ask them where they could take them to that would be a safe place. Then tell them to take them there.

If they cannot think of a safe place, then tell them to wrap them in a white ball of protective light where they will be kept and held safe and protected from all harm – a sort of suspended and pleasurable place, where they can wait until they (the participant) are ready to come back and sort things out. The place can be stocked and coloured according to the preferences of the child – so that the adult can leave them there without guilt or pressure.

The participant who has resolved the situation and committed to the child can bring them with them: **the participant who has been unable to repair the ruptured relationship can leave them safely**, both can then be awakened slowly by returning to the cloud, being awoken, floated back into the work room and counted up to wakefulness.

Although most therapists will be aware of awakening people from such deep states, it must be said that sudden awakening can be traumatic and leave the participant in a fuzzy state of awareness, struggling to fully return to full wakefulness. It is advisable to take time to reverse the visualised process by bringing people back to the cloud and from the cloud back into the room, and then to bring their awareness back into their own physical body before inviting them to open their eyes and counting them upwards to full wakefulness. Even then it is a good idea to check that they feel present, and if they are struggling to take time to count them up to wakefulness again.

Once awake the process can now be debriefed.

The EGG PARENTING exercise is then set up.

ASSIGNMENT: THE EGG AS THE METAPHOR FOR THE VULNERABLE SELF

"When a child is anxious and untrusting, when it has learned that there is nobody to protect or rescue them, when they have blamed themselves and made themselves the flaw, the cause of their own painful experiences in the world, it affects the way they hear promises and proclamations of love. If you adopt an animal that has been subjected to traumatic experiences then it requires careful handling. To win trust again takes time and above all PROOF. So with this egg you are going to explore the condition of your ability to take care of something vulnerable. This egg has the right to be taken care of, to be included and yet to be safe. You are in charge of the safekeeping AND inclusion of this EGG in your life for the next two weeks. You are to have it with you at all times. If it helps you, you can imagine that it is the child you met in your visualisation – but be careful – if you break it, it does not mean that you have broken your child. If you break it, nobody will get hurt at all – the break will be there to teach something about your parental awareness. Making mistakes is how we learn. You will notice things about yourself as you do this. Just notice what you notice. Each time you make a mistake and the egg breaks (if it breaks) replace it with another one as soon as you can and use the previous experience to inform how you go forward together more effectively.

Watch also for what you Meta-Schematic Belief tells you about yourself in this process"

END OF SESSION

The next session begins as always with the question "What is different?"

Once this has been mapped and discussed then the focus turns to the assignment.

"How did you get on with your egg?"

Some will have the original egg, others will have broken theirs any number of times. Spot any evidence of the Meta-Schematic Belief driving self-critical, shaming behaviour – i.e. self-condemnation for being "not good enough" at the assignment and point this out.

Discuss the lessons that are derived from this assignment to establish whether or not they are ready to make a commitment to become the caretaking parent of the child they met in the visualisation of the last session.

If the answer is "yes", then it is time for them to write a love and commitment letter to that same child found in that traumatic situation discovered in the visualization of the last session.

If the answer is "no" then it is not time for the complete commitment, but time to return to the Bill of Rights and the relationships audit.

"What conversation are you not having that would prove to you that you could parent this child in the world." Once this is identified it is time for them to write a letter to the person with whom this conversation is

now due – of course this is a letter that is not necessary to send to the actual living person (if indeed they are alive), the writing of it is often sufficient, however some past participants have rewritten their first attempt and sent it. The letter is really addressing the **introject** – i.e. the internalised person who may represent the original protagonist.

For these participants it is important to stay in the earlier phase of this step until they can make a commitment to the child in the visualisation, at that point they can continue the process as outlined here.

Part two: Rescuing the wounded children.

We can assume that in fulfilling the requirements to move on in the programme the initial visualisation has successfully rescued a wounded version of the participant's early self.

To complete the job we need to ensure that we have begun to win the trust of the earliest possible version of the child. The visualisation is repeated, but this time the participant is regressed to the earliest possible "memory" or internal conceptual self-construction available of a time when they had no rights and this fact was impacting unpleasantly upon them.

We use the same ascending visualisation to achieve this state.

On the cloud they are told that they can 'imagine' the earliest time where they had no rights, no protector/defender and are experiencing the impact of this face in an unpleasant way. Their imagining of it can be something newly remembered or a more detailed version of an old memory – we are not looking at historical accuracy here, we are engaging with the subconscious interpretation of an event that has power over their self-concept. They can accept whatever arises.

They are asked to describe the environment that emerges into their imagination, identify who is there and then describe what is happening *in the present tense..*

Now attention needs to be placed on the victim of the scene –

"What are they feeling?"

"What are they thinking?"

"What belief about their self has been formed already?"

"What is it that you can see on their behalf that they cannot know for themselves from this situation?"

"What would a good parent do in this circumstance to put it right?"

"If a good parent was present in this scene, what would they do?"

"What would the little person here learn from that if it were available?"

After doing all that is necessary to release the child from the situation and its negative impacts they place the child inside their heart and are brought back into wakefulness and presence in the room. This is often accompanied by an expression of emotion with tears.

The egg is now deprogrammed – the child in the egg is removed and placed in the heart of the participant. The egg can then be disposed of in a manner chosen by the participant. It is unwise to eat it! Treating the egg well in its decommissioning is an important issue – it has carried a self-concept and its disposal is significant.

After the process has been debriefed and discussed the assignment is set up.

ASSIGNMENT: *" First write a love letter to the children you have met and rescued as if they are one and the same person. Tell them what they need to know in order to be released from their shame, tell them you commit to being the good parent to them and that you accept them exactly as they are, with all of their fears and feelings; tell them they have rights and tell them exactly what they are (Your Bill of*

Rights for thriving) – tell them you love them. Only when the letter meets all your requirements move on to the second parts of the assignment.

Secondly, record yourself reading it to them into a webcam making sure that your face fills the screen and that you look into the camera as often and for as long as you can. When this is done, sit and imagine yourself as a small child and watch your adult self talking to you and making this commitment. Keep some tissues handy as you may need them. Watch it every day for two weeks."

END OF SESSION

The next session begins as always with the question "What is different?"

Once this has been mapped and discussed then the focus turns to the assignment.

This is a very powerful assignment. The video is watched together with the participant and its effects on the inner conception of the small child explored for improvements in their emotional mood and their levels of trust.

"What qualities do you see in the parent who speaks to you from video?"

These qualities need to be noted for later use in the next step concerned with emerging, authentic ESSENCE. For now the wounded inner child is observing, acknowledging and validating parental qualities in the emerging adult – this is bridging a core relationship breach between the adult and the frozen authentic self conceptualised as the 'child' – the adult is now picking up the crying child who in turn is learning to trust in a virtuous circle. Once this has been achieved the child can begin to guide the adult in exploring the world, growing in skill, and the natural process of development can re-commence yet again. The Authentic Self is unfreezing and the postponed development can begin in earnest assured that enough sustaining parenting is available to it as it changes.

However this is not quite enough to facilitate its total thriving. There are some inner sub-personalities, the enforcers of the Meta-Schematic Blueprint who must be addressed and retired (with love and appreciation) before the process of freely reactivated development can continue.

Three important events must now occur to complete this step.

1) Parents as introjects must be sacked,

2) Guardians of the Meta-Schema must be named and resigned.

3) The functions they fulfilled must be consciously occupied by the participant.

1) SACKING YOUR PARENTS

Hungers are very seductive. When you feel hungry for food for long enough, fantasies of food arise in the imagination. It is what psychoanalysts refer to as Reparative Phantasy. Likewise hungers for parenting. Many participants are still waiting for their mother or father to say *"I am so proud of you"*, *"you're every bit as good as your brother"*, *"I accept your homosexuality"*, *"your different values are perfect for you"*, *"I love the rebel in you",* or for their mother to express the love, acceptance and/or affection that was denied them, to sooth the pain of their divorce, to apologise for the abuse, to create safety that was always denied etc. The desire for the parent to satisfy the deepest hunger can be one of the most difficult and intransigent desires to surrender, and it is one that constitutes one of the most powerful obstacles to freeing the development of the newly activated Authentic Self. I have seen numerous examples of people who have either spent their lives working hard to succeed at the things that their parents most believed they could never excel at; some who have succeeded or failed at the profession that their parent most pushed them into despite the obvious fact that their passions truly lay elsewhere; I have seen numerous people who deliberately sabotaged every success just in case their parents ever allow themselves to believe that they 'did a good job', and so they commit to live their lives as an act of revenge. All of these instances represent states where one party remains hostage to the other and the demand is that an undeclared ransom is paid – and no negotiation has succeeded, no new discipline, no self-help book, no amount of positive affirmation.

Thriving requires the freedom to create what is necessary for thriving to occur – plants in the wrong soil atrophy, become depressed and may even die. So it is with people too. It is not mental illness or an illness, although left long enough it may somatise into disease. It is an emergent property of unmet needs. As said before, humans tend to make themselves wrong for their failure to thrive in the wrong soil – the wrongness is the given, programmed early into the software as a default.

So, to really set about creating the circumstances within which the participant must thrive, it is essential to fire the introjected parents – the Mother and the Father. To be effective this must come with the assured commitment to fulfill the role for oneself, and to share it with others in healthy and supportive, mutually need-meeting relationships.

There is a vitally important distinction here between the introjects and the real world parents.

We are firing the introjects, even though the inner 'parent' concept is derived from experiencing the relationship with the external real world parents. The act of firing the introjects and assuming the roles they were not fulfilling will relieve the expectations on the real world parents. Almost always, the real life parents start to behave differently in unconscious response to the removal of unconscious expectations from their son or daughter as they progress through EMSRP. Setting them free sets the authentic self free in the participant to 'make other arrangements'.

ASSIGNMENT:

"Write two letters each one firing one of your parents regardless of whether or not your real parents are alive or deceased. Tell them that you are taking over the job because you are now a skilled enough parent to do the job well. Let them know whatever you need to express about the impact of their parenting on you. Thank them generously for whatever you are able to be grateful for. Then set them free to be whoever they are."

This assignment can confuse people who consider their real-world relationship with their parents to be functional or better. Sometimes the assessment of their relationship with live parents is mystified – exaggerated in its positive significance as a defense – auditing these relationships can be a struggle for them. The identification of its purpose through a relationship audit will throw light upon this. Parental relationships are the source of guilt and shame as they are FORMATIVE relationships i.e. we are formed out of them. The Meta-Schematic Belief was forged in the fires of this early connection. The impact of unmet hungers and their disappointed, powerless hope that they will somehow be fed appropriately by parents, who have missed them all their lives, is a paralysing situation that prevents other arrangements being made.

By surrendering to the reality that they have been wholly or in part 'barking up the wrong tree', or as one of my past colleagues put it "milking the bull", other more effective arrangements can then be made on behalf of the crying child within. It is to be stressed that only in exceptional circumstance should this letter be sent.

Once the inner sacking has been accomplished, a conversation that makes a difference might be achieved with the real world parents, as in relationship audit stage.

There is usually a significant shift in the relationship with real world parents as a result of this assignment.

END OF SESSION

> *"The most profound event for me in this step was the discovery of a gentle, beautiful and wise place of my psyche that I hadn't given any care and attention to since I was a baby. I became aware as we worked through the module that my rage had become my inner baby's 'protection tank' that was prepared to do anything to shield the vulnerable part of me. Although the raging tyrant inside had done a fantastic job in saving my life in the past and surprisingly was giving me the determination I needed to get back to the gentle part it was also stopping my little voice from being heard. This work gave me the space to notice that the baby inside needed another kind of inner parenting."*

Chapter Six

SACKING THE META SCHEMATIC GUARDIAN
SUBPERSONALITIES

he next session begins as always with the question "What is different?"

Once this has been mapped and discussed then the focus turns to the assignment.

To complete this process the participant is invited to use a Gestalt technique where the individual parent is 'placed on a cushion' and a similar phrase used to accept the individual's Meta-Schematic Belief is said.

"I am willing for you to think that I am worthless, this is not an issue, I am simply going to be myself"

The impact of the reading is then processed and any unfinished business or unsaid issues expressed.

The participant is invited to allow the sacked parent to get up and leave the room if possible in a state of acceptance that they are who they are, and that the relationship is now complete. The parent may be asked if they have a preference for where they would like to be sent, and the participant might prefer to send them somewhere else. In the case of deep wounding, the choice of destination might need to be more deeply thought – a prison, Hell, a place of punishment. They might be erased – however each of these more punitive options carries its own attachment, whether or not placing them there is truly liberating for the participant is something to consider with them. It is rare that, having sacked the parent, participants at this stage want to hold on to them, to continue to exercise punishing or violent retribution against them.

People who can parent themselves well tend to set other people free to be themselves, liberated from any needs-based agenda. Each need can then be negotiated with people who openly consent to mutual need-meeting rather than those who manipulate or are manipulated by others to meet undeclared needs. They become currency for thriving rather than secret and shameful expectations, hopes and anxieties. The ideal is to freely let them go to be who they are – elsewhere if necessary, with the same Bill of Rights for Thriving that the participant has.

Once the parent(s) is (are) sacked, it is time to occupy the space as the best parent for one's own life.

"It's never too late to have a happy childhood".

"As your own parent what is possible that was not possible before? What rules are suspended? How does your energy feel?"

For most people this is a profound moment of freedom. However, some people encounter deep anxiety that they will not be able to do the job adequately.

For both responses it signals the need to do the next process:-
Identifying the guardians of the Meta-Schematic Belief.

2. Naming and Resigning the Guardians of the Meta-Schema.

Consciousness remains one of the most intransigent mysteries in psychology. There have been numerous theoreticians who have attempted to pin it down, but its essence is hard to locate. How is it that the capabilities of conscious awareness arise out of the sum of electrical and bio-chemical impulses native to the matter of the nervous system?

This is not a question for this book. However, perhaps the most useful theory for us to use here for our purposes is to describe Baars Global Workspace Theory of consciousness. Bernard Baars (1997) sees consciousness rather like a stage with lights that remains there unpopulated until characters and objects from the dark and unknown depths of the backstage area emerge into view. Consciousness is not represented by its contents but by the empty stage itself and its capacity to allow objects to dance around on it in full view. This makes the audience able to watch what happens – sometimes to become lost in the stories and happenings, to identify with characters, to be able to shift their experience onto the stage itself.

The EMSRP participant is by now substantially aware that if the Meta-Schematic Belief is not the only 'truth' about what the self is, then there may be an identity beyond that waiting to emerge and that self is an ongoing project to be involved in for the rest of their life. Life and self are not destinations but processes – indeed there may not be a solid and concrete self at all! This can be an alarming thought, and yet the process of development is in truth never ending. The idea that we should become one person and this should be limited because the rules of our Meta-Schematised Beliefs dictate it should by now have no validity, nor should it hold any allure.

New experiences beckon and we begin to explore just how far we can thrive, and what that means in terms of what we do, where we go, what we say 'yes' to, what needs we can meet and get met as we go along, and who we become that is both familiar, as well as new and surprising. There are characters from the past who emerge into the global workspace of our conscious awareness, whose function it is to promote, maintain, enforce and instruct the participant in the Meta-Schematised limitations, and to stay on the course dictated by the blueprint; they protect and preserve the frozen authentic self. Their power has been enhanced by their field of operation being located barely on the edges of consciousness. From here they used the alarm bells of self-doubt, anxiety, anger and shame. Their effectiveness has

121

also depended entirely on our total acceptance that what they say is accurate and important; they want us to never forget we are indeed "worthless", "undeserving", "unlovable", "uniquely flawed".

We have now over the earlier steps challenged every aspect of this belief's validity. The participant has made non-schematic choices, built wider, more permeable boundaries and demonstrated the skills and commitment to announce, defend and enforce them.

The Guardians of the Meta Schematic Blueprint are now to all intents and purposes obsolete – but be in no doubt at all that they are still operational. Their purposeful intention is to keep the participant safe from harm, and in that they are well-intentioned e.g. if expressing my spontaneous joy irritated my alcoholic father to the extent that he beat me to within an inch of consciousness, then treating my joy as the dangerous catalyst to a life-threatening beating was, in that environment, a really smart idea. For me spontaneous joy would always carry a penalty by activating the shaming voices of the Guardian Sub-Personalities, and the self-punishing behaviours that would then ensue. This is an extreme example that is purely illustrative, but other much more subtle examples have equally repressive effects on the ongoing development of a more spacious developing authentic self.

In the spirit of Bernard Baars' useful metaphor, the process begins with a closed eyes process that takes the participant into a theatre to see a show.

The title of the show is **"XXXXXXX (name of participant) Lives the Dream"**

This process can be conducted using hypnosis, or deep relaxation and visualisation, as in the processes dealing with the wounded child earlier in the programme.

In the theatre the participant is asked to take their most preferred seat. They are asked to populate the auditorium with people from their past or present.

A spotlight picks out the child they were and they stand in the shaft of light surrounded by darkness on the stage.

"Your child wants to do something full out and without a care – what is it? They can have anything they want to help them to do it – any equipment, toys, props, costumes, music. They tell you what it is and the audience cheers and claps in support."
"When you child is ready to start, just let me know with a nod of your head."
"The audience is wild with excitement and encouragement."
"Ah, but there's a voice from offstage – trying to put a stop to this – a familiar voice who wants to stop your child fully expressing her/him self."
"What is your child feeling because of this voice?"
"Can you hear it?"
"What is it saying?"
"You stand up in the audience and make your way to the front and up onto the stage – now call the voice out into the lights."
"It has to obey you – insist it comes out from the shadows where you can see it."
"Describe it to me."
"What is its name?"
"Ask it, 'What are you trying to achieve by saying those things?'"

The answers to this final question are very important. Benign intent on the part of each Guardian Sub-Personality is most common.
"Thank them for their service – for doing the best job they could in the circumstance – be really genuinely grateful."
"When you have done that let me know with a nod of your head."

"Explain to (GS Personality's name) why they are no longer needed – explain who you are and what you will do for the child that makes them no longer needed."

"Tell them they are now retired – they can go."

There are a number of alternatives here:

1. Ask the child where they want them sent; the child has been substantially disempowered by the GSP, and this can be very empowering. The child might be given a magic wand to magic them away, or encouraged to shout and stamp their foot and give an order that must be obeyed.

2. Ask the GSP where they want to be sent; the protection of the GSP can sometimes feel especially well-intentioned, even if limiting and misguided. It is a forgiving course of action.

3. Simply allow them to melt into nothing.

Sometimes we come across a GSP that has no discernible benign intent. All GSP's can be removed from service – in this case ask the parent to decide what must be done with it.

"As the parent now decide how you are going to deal with this wholly negative character – they are not there out of reason – they are there to do harm."

"When you have decided what to do simply nod your head."

"Do it now – and when it is gone let me know by nodding your head."

The audience cheer and applaud the exit of the GSP. The parent is asked to tell the child what they need to hear in order to be able to return to their spontaneous performance and for the audience to continue to applaud with delight. Ask them to hear the audience cheering for more.

Repeat the process allowing characters to emerge onto the stage one at a time. Each one is dismissed and the child is given space to express freely.

Each time the important questions are:-

"Who is this character? Describe them."

"What is their name?"

"How does he/she/it think he/she/it is helping, protecting or preserving little you?"

"What does he/she need to hear to accept that you are safe without them?"

It is rare to find more than four or five clearly distinctive characters. However, even in those cases there are usually two main protagonists who are assisted by others. One character assesses and judges the world and the other condemns and shames the participant. For example, one female participant (AA) had a female Sub-Personality who embodied total fear and hatred of men and pushed AA to attack any male who got too close. AA's greatest desire was to be married with children, and this sub-personality cheated her of this into her late 30's. AA also had a male sub-personality who swore at her, name-called and shamed her whenever she did anything spontaneous, self-serving or different. He was a version of an abusive stepfather who had died in her adolescence, but who, as an introject, had been wrought over time and perfected into a slick and efficient, punishing enforcer.

Once AA had seen these clearly, named them, heard their voices, and let them know that they were no longer needed, their subsequent attempts to subvert her progress weakened and her own self-parenting skills strengthened. Life and AA transformed.

She can now spot these in a flash and is highly sensitised to other peoples guardian sub-personality driven behaviours. She is currently in a loving relationship with a man and they are planning to have children together.

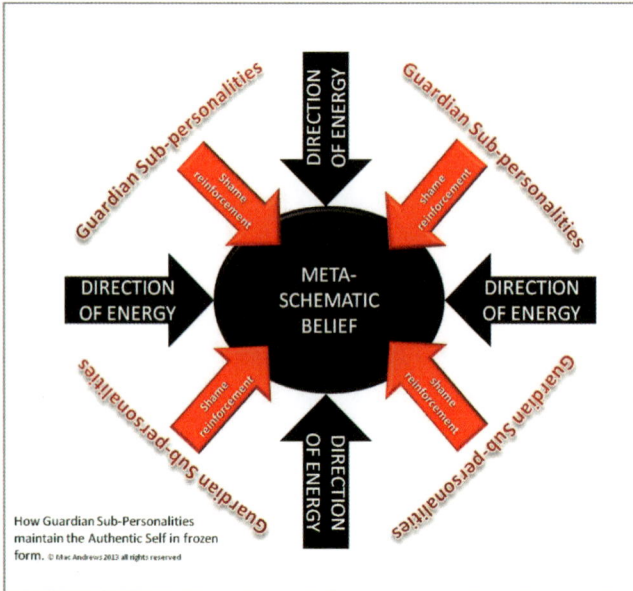

How Guardian Sub-Personalities maintain the Authentic Self in frozen form. © Mac Andrews 2013 all rights reserved

In this first graphic map to the left you can see how the guardian sub-personalities maintain the frozenness of the Authentic Self by reinforcing the Meta-Schematic Belief through shaming self-talk. All behaviours that are put out into the social world are therefore highly censored, pretested and controlled. The energy is inwards that leads to self absorption, self-consciousness and ultimately depression.

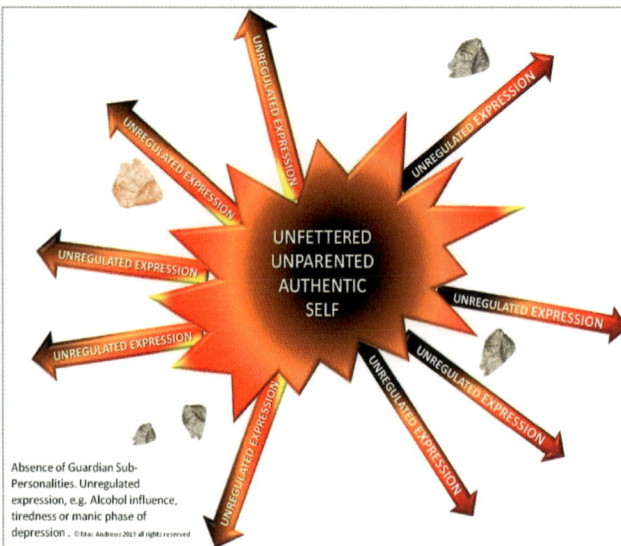

Absence of Guardian Sub-Personalities. Unregulated expression, e.g. Alcohol influence, tiredness or manic phase of depression. © Mac Andrews 2013 all rights reserved

This second graphic illustrates the manic outburst. At times when the guardian sub-personalities are not active, knocked out by alcohol, tiredness or a "fuck it" decision, the brakes come off completely and energy is put out into the world with unregulated abandon. The guardians come rushing back in – periods of spontaneity are marked by an increase in the intensity of the shame- reinforcing voices. *"Oh my God what the f*** are they all going to think of you?"* *"You didn't say that did you. You stupid, worthless idiot!"* and so on in that vein.

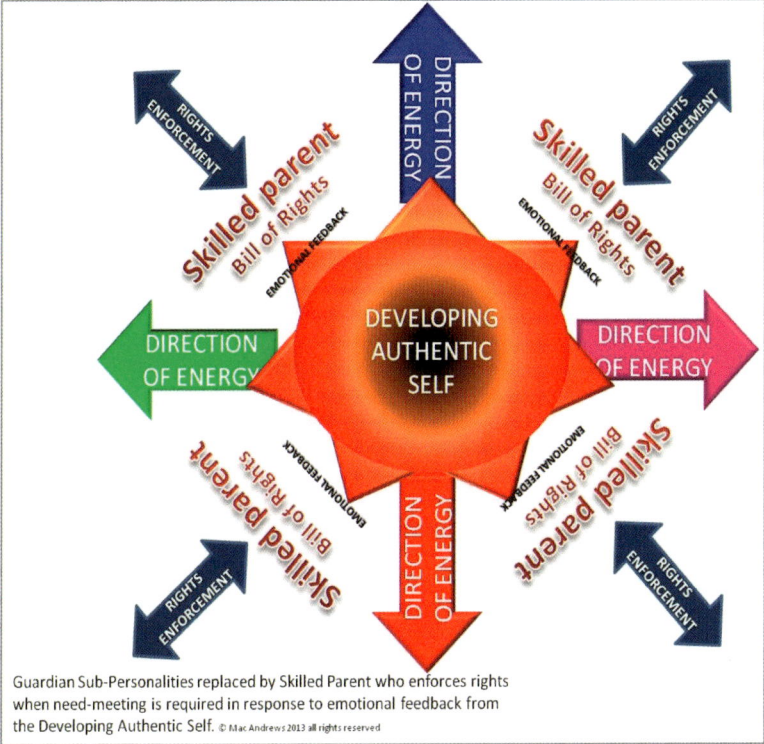

Guardian Sub-Personalities replaced by Skilled Parent who enforces rights when need-meeting is required in response to emotional feedback from the Developing Authentic Self. © Mac Andrews 2013 all rights reserved

In this third graphic, above, the Skilled Parent replaces the Guardian Sub-personalities. The parent is responsible and able to enforce rights where needed and to navigate the social world in order to facilitate the needs of the Developing Authentic Self. As the world is negotiated in new ways emotions become the temperature gauges for assessing how the project of development is going – e.g. anger flags up threats to wellbeing, sadness the loss of important people and objects, depression indicates needs being missed and joy accompanies flow etc. The direction of life energy is *out* into the world. Any residual presence of voices of shame from Guardian Sub-personalities becomes evidence of spontaneity in novel environments, and good parenting identifies these voices increasingly speedily and replaces them with supportive self-feedback. My mother believed me to be "off the rails" as she put it. Her rails were such that to be "off" them was a good indicator that I was living my life without being ruled by fear and her dysfunctional restraints. Like the Guardian Sub-Personality voices, she provided some evidence that I was on my own track. Likewise if you have done something different, something new and pleasurable, or stood up for your rights for thriving, the Guardian Sub-Personalities will kick off. Shame is evidence that you lived beyond their limitations. Good news. If there is anything real to clean up, you can do so and still love yourself!

In EMSRP we refer to this dynamic mechanism that senses the world and feeds back through emotional responses the Thrivometer. Depressive symptoms express through the Thrivometer so that action can be taken to increase the Thrivometer reading. Anti-depressant medications subvert the Thrivometer and the symptoms cease to be available to measure and emotional energy is damped and is lost as the resource for action-taking in the environment that it provides. Anti depressants and anti anxiety medications are almost always merely a sticking plaster, drug induced anaesthetics that permits the depleting conditions to persist. **This is not a recommendation to stop taking medication if you are already on it** – you must always seek the guidance of a qualified medical practitioner before altering your medication. However, getting free of anti-depressant medication responsibly is a worthy objective in pursuit of thriving. If you choose to do it, only do it under professional guidance.

END OF SESSION

Chapter Seven
ALL THINGS ESSENCE

At the beginning of this step it is important to inform the participant that it is the final part of the programme and that when they present their work they will graduate. Most of the participants we have seen are ready to leave as they are already experiencing positive changes around and inside them. It is a core objective that participants become independent, and able to create interdependent relationships in which all parties thrive. However, sessions are deeply intimate, with boundaries to make the intimacy safe, and satisfying as many deficiency needs are met by the relationship. Maintaining firm appointments and spotting 'foot-dragging' at this point is wise, as participants can procrastinate in order to perpetuate their relationship with you.

ALIGNING WITH ESSENCE

Successful completion of all previous steps means that the Authentic Self is now substantially actively developing beyond the limits of the Meta-Schematic Belief and its blueprint.

The question *"What is different?"* will be harvesting many rich observations by now. The aim of Step Seven is to align self-parenting with the now re-developing Authentic Self. Themes evident in this emerging Authentic Self's innate desires to take form through the life and in the world of the participant are becoming more evident.

The psychological cliché of Abraham Maslow's Hierarchy of Needs (Maslow, 1943) is useful here. Maslow's idea was that we have deficiency needs (needs that require repeated maintenance) that are prioritised according to their place on a hierarchical ladder.

The needs at the lower levels must be sufficiently satisfied for us to be free to address those at higher levels. (See illustration below)

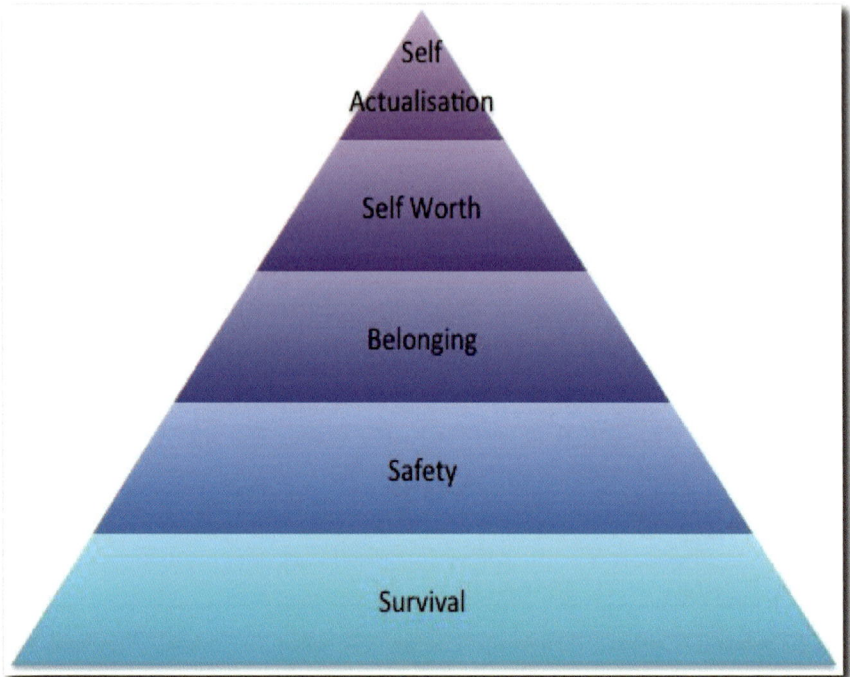

In the main they must be dealt with in specific order. Thus in the bottom segment of the pyramid, physiological survival deficiency needs must be taken care of for us to fully engage in dealing with safety needs at the next level in the segment above; safety needs dealt with before belonging, belonging needs before esteem and so on. Anyone will know that when you are so thirsty that you feel you might faint, your self-esteem is not the urgent priority. Likewise, during those tricky years at school, being socially excluded might lead anybody to sacrifice their self-esteem for the feeling that they are accepted somewhere, anywhere, even by the lowest status social group, or even becoming part of the bully's 'gang'. When the Meta-Schematic Belief holds the participant in a low place in the hierarchy, belonging, self-esteem and certainly self-actualisation seem very remote, even impossible hungers indeed.

In reactivating the development of the Authentic Self through EMSRP we have also substantially begun the process of need-meeting. These unmet needs will queue up in conscious awareness for satisfaction. Unlike the words of Mick Jagger, through this process you certainly *can* and *do* get satisfaction.

As relationships transform or fall away and are replaced by interactions that lead to and support thriving, self-esteem grows, as testimonials and the growing body of data from previous EMSRP participants verify.

The pinnacle of the pyramid, Self-Actualisation, gradually becomes an attainable prospect. Self-Actualisation is a poorly understood concept. This is not surprising since most of us are denied any experience of this from our earliest years by the culturally ubiquitous Meta-Schematic Blueprint for our lives, which keeps us hungry at the lower levels of need in Maslow's hierarchy. A self-actualised environment is one that mirrors back to us what we experience ourselves to be, in the essence of "me". When I am self-actualised, that which 'I am', is found to surround me and reflect authentic 'me' back.

Now, you could argue that self-actualisation is a universal law inasmuch as the *frozen* authentic self in effect actualises itself in the environment by being driven to construct its *opposite* in the world – the NOT-ME is an expression of it, albeit in reverse. The "worthless" self perfectly expresses a self-image, a sophisticated NOT-ME; without the NOT-ME the only alternative is to present worthlessness as a badge of honour, a martyred self, which some people do. Specialness as a flawed human, "Nobody is as flawed as me" can provide a last haven for the ashamed, but is a peculiarly lonely place. To accept others as flawed loses them their unique status. Competitive flawedness is a particularly pernicious form of self-shaming.

EMSRP, on the other hand, leads to the self-actualisation of an emerging and dynamically developing self into relationships, into environments, into career, hobby, style, life-emphasis etc. all of which support all other levels of the need hierarchy on an ongoing basis – in short it supports thriving.

So this begs the questions **"What is trying to express?"**, **"Which bit is truly ME?"** and crucially **"What is the essence of my me-ness?"**

What or who is essence?

Benjamin Libet (1985), at the University of California, did a pivotally important and elegantly simple experiment. He wired up peoples brains with sensors starting at the lowest part of the brain where unconscious activity prevails, through the mid brain and onwards up to the higher cortices (the big walnut-like hemispheres) where our more sophisticated processing and conscious activity occurs.

He asked people to move their index finger at random intervals.

Now something amazing happened.

To fully appreciate what occurred, you need to understand something about activity in the brain. For anything to happen in the brain neurons have to fire. Electrical charges, called action potentials, have to be activated and repeated. The more firing that occurs in a greater number of neurons, the more powerfully detectable by conscious awareness the impulse becomes. In other words neuronal firing has to achieve a certain level of intensity for the activity to reach our conscious awareness – a lot of firing has to go on for this to happen. Most firing in the brain happens at levels way below the level required for us to be aware of it.

Libet discovered that the impulse to move the finger happened at a level way below the possibility for conscious awareness – and took about a third of a second to achieve a level of firing that allowed it to become conscious. That meant that the impulse happened *before* conscious awareness. **This is a big finding!**

Now a quarter of a second might not seem very long at all in the grand scheme of things. But in neuroscience this is a *long* time. It means that the decision to move the finger was not a conscious decision at all – the decision arose first somewhere *unconscious*.

This has led neuroscientists to wonder if there are any decisions we make that are achieved consciously. In fact they have long been questioning whether there is any such thing as 'free will' as we have learned to think about it.

The Harvard Psychologist Daniel Wegner (Wegner and Wheatley, 1999: Wegner, 2002) believes that conscious will is illusory (See illustration on page 134)

He proposes that, "the experience of conscious will arises when a person infers an apparent causal path from thought to action. The actual causal paths are not present in the person's consciousness. The thought is caused by unconscious mental events, and the action is caused by unconscious mental events, and these unconscious mental events might also be linked to each other directly or through yet other mental or brain processes. Conscious will is experienced as a result of what is apparent, not what is real."

The decision is made somewhere – but where?

So who or what is making the decision?

So here's a thing –

As a baby you flowed without physical or mental skills.

As you flowed you experimented and noticed what happened, and you naturally adjusted yourself and your world without thinking about it.

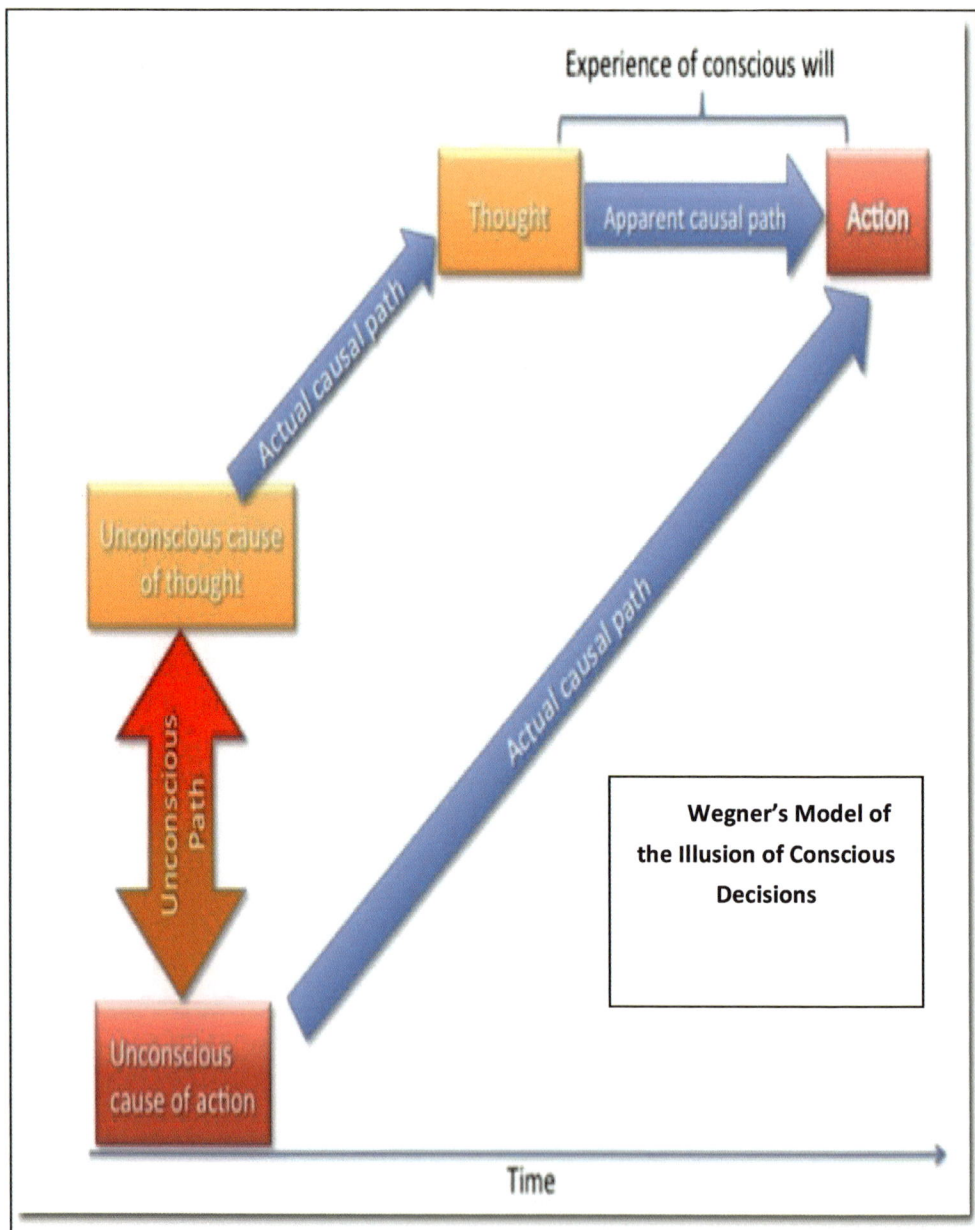

Experience of conscious will

Thought — Apparent causal path → Action

Actual causal path

Unconscious cause of thought

Unconscious Path

Unconscious cause of action

Actual causal path

Wegner's Model of the Illusion of Conscious Decisions

Time

The flow of you-ness just kept going until you got tired or were diverted by a need. There was no distance between the energy and the expression. You flowed and you watched and learned from it.

Then things happened where the world started to enforce itself on you, and you were called to locate your self somewhere other than in your flow, you had to separate from your flow – you had to become *conscious about what you were doing.* From a state where all decisions were made unconsciously and resulted in instant to flow, the world gradually called your attentional resources into conscious awareness of yourself. Being your flow and allowing your flow to use all of your resources became dangerous and you had to begin to work out how to do stuff that was not flow-driven, or simply not do flow driven stuff at all.

You stepped out of flow to regard the impacts of your being-in-flow on others who called for you to **"stop"**, or **"be different"**, or took you from your instant **"doing from being"** into **"don't do from 'being' – do from consideration of other factors."** You became conscious of the things you were doing and the impacts that those things taught you that might lead you to have unpleasant, mortifying or even seemingly life-threatening experiences. Your "doing from being" energy became an energy to "think about" before acting. A new "you" emerged inside your conscious awareness – amassed out of the contents of your consciousness. The "you" that emerged our of the dark cave of your unconsciousness, the already decided energy trying to flow to become something in the world got stopped by the "you" created out of consciousness. That is what you then identified with as your identity – the CONSCIOUS you. That old 'you', the one that emerged quite naturally and freely as flow became dangerous to the new you that was conscious of itself. You were evicted from your Garden of Eden.

You ruptured your conscious self from your own flow. Your essence was held in check. You disowned your flow – "totally unlike me".

Essence is pregnant with directional intent – put another way, you already decided what came next. You cut your conscious awareness, and all of your personal powers became denied to the core you energy. Essence couldn't practice manifesting itself any more, it could not rehearse and re-rehearse, it could not inject itself freely into the world because YOU JOINED IN WITH THE PARENTING THAT STOPPED IT. So when it did burst out, it lacked skill, nuance, craft, maturity, it made messes to be cleared up, it became the enemy.

Here is the most important EMSRP 'truth' of all truths.

You are your essence.

The new supportive parent is simply **a tool to bridge your essence into the world,** to introduce him/her, to smooth the path, to facilitate the structures. The child only exists in your psyche because he/she got separated from and shamed for the source essence, shamed for the clumsy and unskilled early attempts to shape the world into forms that satisfied the already-decided essence. The parent is only required when the Thrivometer senses threat, obstacle or indicates that flow has been interrupted. Listening to the messages of the vulnerable self (the child communicating using the language of emotions) enables the nurturing parent (the Bill of Rights plus the willingness to construct the conversation or actions that will make the difference) to restore flow. You as essence can then flow unhindered, unshamed, lending all of your resources to the fulfillment of the innate already-present desires of essence as you emerge form the darkness of the unconscious onto the lighted stage of awareness.

So if I think I am something other than my essence, how do I step back into it again?

Well, that is the profound purpose of this final stage. It is the greatest gift of EMSRP.

I want to stress at this point, this is not spiritual nor is it religious in EMSRP. It is entirely pragmatic, scientific and tangibly real. Those who interpret what occurs naturally in humans as spiritual or religious do so for their own reasons. To me it is simply the natural inheritance of us in the scheme of human development, no more, no less.

Meeting your essence.

Essence is a quintessential remnant of anything when all the extraneous stuff is stripped away. Michael Maynard of Maynard Leigh Associates talks about essence displaying itself in the difference between the *feel* of people as they create. He suggests imagining different people singing the same song, for example Boiled Beef and Carrots, let's say Mick Jagger (seeing how I used him earlier), The Cheeky Girls (Google them if you have no idea who they were), Barack Obama and the Dalai Lama. Each person's rendition of Boiled Beef and Carrots would be unique even though the song is identical. I am encountering people I haven't seen since school days a little over forty years ago, and each time I notice that something of their essence is still perceptible, even they have had to adjust and reform themselves over time in response to the specific circumstance their lives have thrown at them.

In psychology, the science of psychometrics has endeavoured to pin down and measure the elements of individual difference. To measure what a person IS, we need to be able to distinguish between an individual's dynamic **states** that may not last long, and **traits,** that are stable over time and in a range of different environments. So to illustrate this, I have noticed that my kids' states change in different subjects at school – my youngest (now 15) is alive and enthusiastic in Art, Design and Creative Textiles, and restless, frustrated and disengaged in Geography. She exhibits a spectrum of states across the subjects, and her Geography teacher is horrified when I tell him that she is simply not going to be a 'Geographer' and that I have no interest in trying to persuade her to feign geographical passions, and even less in forcing her to push herself through the subject at GCSE. Her essence drives her enthusiastic attention towards some things and not others. She thrives in the production of objects that she can stand back and admire, that have a style that embody her spirit, and this endeavour draws her into ceaseless refinement of skills without any resistance at all. Art and design, creativity expressed through her hands simply light her up. Her stable traits of essence express both in Geography through her lack of any interest whatsoever and her tight frustration (something alive and keen is being frustrated after all) and creative, artistic and artisan activities (something alive and keen is being released). Her ESSENCE exhibits character behind her expression. Each of my children is unique in their essence, my wife in hers, me in mine. I hasten to add that they all have Xboxes and Playstations, but they use them sparingly. There is no purpose in displacement activity when essence meets acceptance and appropriate resources to flow. When essence is defeated, denied and impossible, the escape into anesthesia becomes an entirely reasonable destination for relief from the pain of being divorced from the source of yourself. Essence NEEDS expression – it is primal. Without it we inevitably become directionless. No wonder kids spend days and nights staring into screens, escaping from the widespread subjugation of their essence! Being forced to be what you are not before you have a chance to explore what you might be given the room to find out is intolerable – and depressing, anxious, frustrating and leads to loathing of the world and self. No wonder then that self-harm is increasing.

How many people arrive in therapy to state – *"I feel as if I am in the wrong life/job/relationship/house/groups...."*?

The greatest gifts from within are disregarded, disowned and feared; frustration, envy, sadness, depression – the richest of signposts towards essence and its already decided intentionality, the routes towards satisfaction and ultimate self-actualisation, are being denied, outlawed, numbed, medicated or masked by both individual and culturally collective commitment to the Meta-Schematic Belief and its Guardians. Now that participants are sensitised to these signposts, it is time to identify their personal traits of essence and to align their permissions and rights in living with and above all EXPRESSING them.

Essence never died regardless of the sophisticated levels of resistance to it. **It leaked out in places where there had been no focus on it. But because these moments of essence received no focus from others, negative or positive, to invalidate or validate it, what essence was trying to be 'up to' became of no importance.** The 'urgent' issue in those past times was whether NOT-SELF was working as a complete smoke-screen or not, and whether or not sufficient needs were being met to at least survive and get by. Essence is there, it always has been, and it turns up with us everywhere we go. People have seen it, but are unlikely to have ever spoken about it. Even if they have, it is unlikely we ever took in what they said and fed ourselves with it.

Essence, *real-you*, is trying to be 'up to something' by expressing through behaviours that suit your authentic agenda – to express into forms in the world. What real-you is up to may never have been given the opportunities necessary to practice, rehears, fail, try again and bit by bit mature and develop into full expression. But real-you is always there, still undeveloped, latent and waiting for a better day.

So when people arrive to seek help with their lives they often say, "I do not know who I am". The answer? Well, who you are hasn't happened yet; you are a dynamic and developing, ever changing and responding essence trying to take forms in the ever changing physical world, and you will never stop changing and developing if you create the appropriate care for yourself as you become aware of your essence driving you forward. Real-you cannot be "known" until he/she is allowed to emerge without interference into conscious awareness, welcomed there, accepted as he/she is, then nurtured into being through flow, and finally implemented in the outer world.

Once upon a time you led yourself to believe that you were your smokescreen NOT-SELF, until it failed and you were left believing that you were only really your frozen, un-developing Authentic Self defined by your Meta-Schematic Belief; in fact you were split into two polar opposites, and at one end lay hollow hope and the other depressing despair.

It is now time to address this question:- "What is *my* essence?" Note at this point, I am talking to your conscious mind and thus refer to essence as "it", when really it is YOU. For now I have to do this to avoid confusing your conscious mind.

Essence is something unfamiliar that we cannot see for ourselves, thus we are going to need help to bring it into our own awareness and accept it with open arms. Essence has impact i.e. it makes changes in and impacts upon the outside forms of the world. Objective forms include other human beings who experience the impact of essence *subj*ectively. Essence makes subjective impressions. This assignment involves becoming a researcher for a while and asking people about what they experience our essence to be!

Whilst we may have spent many years trying to assess whether our Meta-Schematic impression management was effective or not, we will have little or no idea as to what this new honesty will create. This research will feel really vulnerable to both parties in the interaction, and will require excellent parenting if we are going to elicit quality responses from our interviewees. Our old way usually only informed us about how we were doing when we failed, and reminded us to obscure how bad we really were much more effectively in the future when our worthlessness, as we could assess it, was exposed. A shaming episode could have been triggered by a look, a moment of paranoia, a word, a facial expression from someone else and the proof that we had failed to keep up appearances was perceived by us staring back at us in the mirror.

But you can be sure that your Essence turns up with you everywhere you go. Despite you hiding it, people feel it, sense it and, without putting it into words, will unconsciously reference it when identifying you as someone distinct from others. Not only that, essence, as stated above, only continues its unfettered expression in areas of life that remained unnoticed by authority figures and unsupportive peers from the past. Their critical attention legitimised whatever was being focused on through punishments and rewards, both obvious and subtle. Your high scores in science may have been prized and your success in art may have been barely noticed.

So we have to pin down essence in its unnoticed forms, playgrounds and, by researching its impacts in the social world by recording its impacts on other people.

Because our culture tends to train people not to share such observations with others this will demand a different sort of conversation than we are most used to, even this far in EMSRP. It is generally easier to ask others for criticism, good advice or agenda-driven flattery and expect to receive it in abundance about ourselves than it is to ask about the honest themes of our essence. So selecting the people to ask in this research with some discernment is important.

We need people who are 'for' us, and here we need to introduce a new concept.

The Importance of For-ness.

We introduce participants to the idea of 'for-ness'. Along the way through EMSRP some relationships may have proven to be supportive of thriving, at least in parts, and may already be transforming into being more supportive and beneficial to the task of thriving. Somebody who is 'on your side' in your success could be said to be 'for' you. Their 'for-ness' would be high. Somebody who thrives at your expense by, for example, metaphorically cutting your head off to make *them* look taller by constantly one-upping every success you share, and making your successes seem insignificant by comparison, would be displaying low 'for-ness' for you. Why would we choose to substitute 'for-ness' for words like 'support' or 'friendship'? Well words matter. My good friend Roy Langmaid, from whom I inherited the concept of 'forness', talks about the 'fat' words we use in life, that are thrown around in conversation like "salad" with the assumption that each time they are used they represent exactly the same thing. An example of this is how sometimes we might use the word 'support' to mean agreement with a point of view, another time it might represent a hug, another time it might represent an undeclared expectation that someone else should take the strain. Two people in assuming that the word has the same meaning for both concurrently are likely to misinterpret each other and wind up at cross purposes. The distinction 'for-ness' describes accurately the phenomenon we seek to identify in others that qualifies them to participate in the research.

Setting up the assignment.

Facilitator: *"Think of someone who is high in 'for-ness' in your life, or who you think is open to being that way for you."* If the participant who understands the idea of 'for-ness' struggles then the facilitator can use themselves as an example.

Facilitator: *"Give me a for-ness score out of 10 where 0 would be totally against you, 5 would be indifferent and 10 would be totally on your side in your success in life."*

As the facilitator you might reasonably expect to have a high score. You can then ask them how they know this to be the case – to identify some of the characteristics of 'for-ness'. Once they have done this ask them to identify people who display some of these characteristics or who might well display them given the opportunity. Tell them that a good parent would not put their child into a conversation like this with someone who was against them.

Once they have identified as many people as they can (including you) then turn to the conversation they need to have with those candidates to set up this unusual interaction. By this stage of the EMSRP process they should be able to create this for themselves.

Facilitator: **"Bearing in mind that you are asking people the question "What is my essence?", and that they are unlikely at first to know for certain what you mean by this, this is likely to feel like a risky conversation for both of you. What do you need to say to them to set it up in order to make it as safe as possible for them to give you what you are asking for? Create the script for the conversation so** *that the other person has all the permission they need, and they are as clear as possible about the task. Bear in mind that they have the same rights as you."*

After some time writing their script, the facilitator gives them the opportunity to try it out in a rehearsal with them.

The facilitator gives the participant feedback about what is missing for them to feel really safe to give them the kinds of responses they seek, and this information is used to edit the script until it feels robust.

The facilitator uses the participant's script to ask the participant to feedback about the facilitator's essence. Once the participant and facilitator agree that it feels inviting and safe for both parties then the participant gets to give feedback to the facilitator about *their* essence.

The facilitator hears each piece of feedback and repeats it aloud, says 'thank you' and writes it down. If the participant strays into good advice, veiled or blatant criticism the facilitator needs to observe this, indicating the impact this has, and role model how to deal with it without blame or condemnation.

"Another time that (good advice or criticism) might be useful, but for this exercise I just need my essence as you perceive it. What is it about me that makes me uniquely me – that would make me someone different if it wasn't there?"

Once it is robust, the facilitator gives feedback about the participant's essence from their point of view.

Feedback needs to be kept simple and generous, whilst truthful and not over-justified or over-explained. The facilitator is giving back into the ownership of the participant qualities of self that are not available to them any other way. They, as facilitator, must be careful that eagerness for the participant to be successful through EMSRP does not colour their feedback and thereby flatter them (the facilitator) by default. Remember too that your client/participant has had a lifetime of disowning, rejecting, invalidating, even condemning their essential self. They are likely to require a deal of encouragement, reassurance and role modeling of acceptance for gifts like these.

Whilst one participant might attract observations like "mischievous, iconoclastic and self-searching", another might be "sensitive to others' limits, empathic and perceptive". Many words may come or few, images might emerge into consciousness and in that case share the image, poetry may come to mind, music, weather, animals; the essence, when all behaviour is stripped away, may inspire all sorts of media for its communication into forms that can contain, represent and communicate it. This is an opportunity to bring into view not only essence, but also how it expresses through the 5 powers of personality, i.e. **intellect, imagination, perception, emotions** and **will**.

To offer "your blue eyes" is always irrelevant, despite the fact that they might turn up with them everywhere they go!

It is vital that the participant writes down everything they hear fed back to them whether they agree with it or not – agreement or disagreement are immaterial. They also need to include criticism and 'good advice' if it occurs, and this can be identified, analysed and separated from the essence statements in the following session. Learning to separate the resources for thriving from the other 'stuff', the food for the NOT-ME, is an important skill.

ASSIGNMENT:

"Conduct as many interviews as you can manage before the next session. Note down accurately word-for-word, all of the responses you get without trying to work out what they mean. Notice what you notice."

144

END OF SESSION

The next session begins as always with the question "What is different?"

Once this has been mapped and discussed then the focus turns to the assignment.

All of the feedback from the essence research is sifted through and mapped for themes — the participant is asked which elements of essence most surprised them, that were good news, any which confirmed expectations or suspicions, and those that felt like bad news. Any criticism or good advice that has leaked into the list needs to be identified and discarded. The themes that emerge are identified displayed on a single page.

The core and most common obstacle to grasping essence is identification with the NOT-SELF. If the participant is preoccupied with seeking evidence from their research with which they agree or disagree, then this is sufficient evidence that they have not grasped the concept. Essence simply IS, as we already know. It does not care what anyone thinks about it or believes it should be. Its presence is evidenced in the EFFECTS that it CAUSES. In relationship it will CAUSE experiential EFFECTS in others. Bear in mind that most people are out of touch with what happens inside their bodies in terms of emotionally physiological effects. Those energies that intrude from within tend to be made sense of out of the Meta-Schematic Belief, and we have to be careful how the results from this research are framed and what they are taken to mean. The MSB is preoccupied with maintaining the shame based status quo, and with motivating the behaviours that most obscure the worst self-concept thus preventing it from being revealed. The question *"What makes me the unique individual I am?"* is likely to provoke feedback filtered and guided by the MSB driven agendas of the interviewees. EMSRP is about thriving, not criticism or good-advice.

Here is a sample set of feedback from a real participant.

"Your facial expressions are what make you you, none of your pictures can capture your aliveness".

"Your contagious cheerfulness!! Even when you are sad you are cheery about it! I just see you and I feel happy".

"There are happy people, and there are sad people. Then there is a Christina (name altered for anonymity) level of optimism that no one else can ever achieve".

"You are an optimistic realist. You believe in the good of everyone, yet you are not ignorant to realities".

"You are determined and passionate, you are a motivator".

"You are very adaptable".

"Too loveable, not egocentric. You don't approach conversations with the intention of making yourself look good".

"You don't seek personal benefit at the expense of others".

"Quirky, in a good way; You are not typical. You have a very special outlook on life that is entirely unique".

"Imaginative! You are fucking hilarious – you have an extremely unique, dark, dramatic, morbid and twisted sense of humour, yet childish and innocent – who else wants to be an avocado plant, breed dinosaurs, keep my brain in a jar, and grow mould so she can kill it?".

"Dramatic!"

"Charming and uplifting – you have an elegance in the way you hold yourself and move, and burst into song like the world is a charming musical".

There may be an interesting piece of veiled good advice/criticism that emerges from the MSB behavioural blueprint in the statement, *"Too loveable, not egocentric".* The subliminal resonance with the participant's MSB as "I am worthless" makes it a fertile remark for paranoia. It does not take too much imagination to start hearing what the Guardian Sub Personalities might make of that statement – *"See I told you so, nobody believes you. You're fucking worthless and the sooner you get back to listening to me the better. Firing me!! Blah blah blah".*

This participant had accepted her need to isolate herself as a result of her exhaustion from serving the needs of others, not to feel good about it, but to minimise her feelings of shame. She had adopted the concept of Introversion to explain this. However, since learning about entering social settings without a plan and trusting her Thrivometer and Bill of Rights, she had begun to witness the effect she was having even when not activating any attempts at social control. The themes that emerge in this small sample of her extensive list of data from her research, display some key themes.

"Aliveness, optimism, passion, motivation , quirky with a unique outlook, uplifting, funny, charming, elegant." Speaking as this participant's facilitator, I can vouch for the accuracy of this list.

Male or female, you can begin to build an inner picture of what this person, living this essence to the fullest extent, might look like, do for a living, their style, their leisure pursuits, the living spaces they might create for themselves, the relationships they might thrive most inside. These qualities of essence are evident in their experiential effects on others.

When invited to share those effects, this is the sort of feedback this participant harvested. They are the effects of a cause – and the cause originates in the energy of her essence.

In EMSRP, we believe that essence is "I". Essence when embedded in the world becomes "Me". At this level of my being, I am what I am. The question "What am I?" tends to lead to self-definition in other terms. But the inquiry, "Who am I?" is bogus. "Who am I? comes form the needs of the conscious self to be in total control of how he/she appears to others. "Who am I" is not in conscious awareness – it appears from the unconscious. I cannot know all that I am when it is in flow with the chaos of causes and effects that surround me at all times, and which I am forced to negotiate my way through. Imagine white water rushing through a canyon. The dynamic causes and effects at play in any one moment are innumerable and immeasurable, the next moments each previous cause is reaping billions of effects that in turn cause more billions of effects and so on. Anything rigid in that water will be battered, broken and reformed by its forces. The reality of living is that we are in the flow, and a rigid self-concept will be tested, battered and ultimately, if it has no flexibility, it will be forced to bend until it fails. This point of failure is commonly called a "breakdown". In EMSRP this point is a break*through.*

Essence is uncompromisingly itself, and it needs to meet a welcoming and adaptive vehicle as it meets the awkward forces of the external world. The conscious mind's powers – the will, imagination, perception, emotions and intellect, as well as the body must be on its side, aligned to essence's purpose. The conscious mind has held essence hostage, or repelled it as an enemy to survival. Conscious awareness, such as it was in early life, created and got caught up in a Meta Schematic Belief and a crude behavioural blueprint in the first years of life, in order that each of us could get through the adverse conditions for thriving presented to us; it did this in the hope of a better day. Essence wants to be up to something – what we think of as "me" simply won't let it.

Now these energies are being released, "Who I am" becomes an exponential, creative project. The better question for essence is *"Who is my essence trying to become right now?"* or *"What is my Essence trying to be up to?"*

Who I am, once my Authentic development is restarted, develops all the time.

The Person Essence Wants to Become.

This process may be conducted as a closed-eyes exercise. Experience has told us that a full-scale hypnosis session may not be needed but is not proscribed in any sense.

Facilitator:- *"Imagine you are going through the possessions of an unknown person in order to find out as much about them as possible and you stumble across this information about them somewhere in a box. Allow your imagination free rein as you allow them to emerge into your mind –*

- *What do you know about them?*
- *What kind of life do you think they lead if they are truly expressing all these qualities?*
- *What sorts of friendships do they cultivate?*
- *What do they do for pleasure?*
- *Where do they live?*
- *What do they do for their living?*
- *What hobbies do they have?*
- *Take in the colours, feelings, sounds, and environments of this person.*
- *Now ask yourself 'What is this person really up to?" remember the answer if you get one"*

When the visualisation or conversation is concluded, the participant is given time to draw pictures, write notes and record everything that they saw and felt. The answer to the question *"What is this person really up to?"* is very important. In EMSRP we have seen years of evidence that essence is 'up to something' despite all efforts at suppressing it.

The author's essence is up to "the rediscovery of innocence". This is what my essential energy is 'up to'. It is the source of EMSRP, my parenting of my own children, my love for my wife, and for my liberated Authentic Self. It directs my path, it bought me my kite as an adult and it polishes and rides my beautiful Triumph motorcycles, it contextualises my view of people as fundamentally innocent and driven to poor choices through the unmet needs of the frozen Authentic Self. It is present in my work, my interests, my reading, my spare time activities, my dreams and everything I turn up to somehow or other is coloured by it when I am fear free.

Essence is the quintessential energy that hangs it all together, and what is so wonderful about it, is that it turns up with me wherever I go. It needs no preparation as it has always been there, and in researching it I, and many participants, discovered that people have sensed it all

149

along. It never died despite all attempts at obscuring it, repressing it, compensating for a believed lack of it, our own non-acceptance and rejection of it.

Essence turns on when we are awake and off when we sleep. And when our needs are met on an ongoing basis it can express freely knowing it is being well parented by its possessor. EMSRP transforms it from being the source of our shame and abandonment to being the signpost to our thriving and growth.

The inner images and experiences of the person living as essence are reference points for the participant in identifying how they might self-actualise, or put another way, to create a world that matches and mirrors their inner developing Authentic Self. The emerging newly developing Authentic Self is not fixed – it is growing and developing always. So the self-actualised world is not fixed either – the participant at 30 will be grown even further by 35 and further still by 40.

ASSIGNMENT

"Using the results from your visualisation, audit your life using the following questions: -

1) *What is already in place in my life that matches the life I witnessed in my visualisation?*
2) *What is stuck in my life that is preventing its flow into alignment with my essence?*
3) *What is obsolete, irrelevant and exhausting me?*
4) *What is missing the presence of that would make the most difference?*
5) *How am I holding back from what my essence wants to be 'up to'?*

Bring the results of this audit to the next session in three-four weeks"
END OF SESSION

The next session begins as always with the question "What is different?"

Once this has been mapped and discussed then the focus turns to the assignment.

The results of the assignment are always ripe with insight. The aim of this step is to shift the locus of identity form parent /child to Essence, and from that shift to view life as a vehicle for its flow into the world.

Now it is common, indeed desirable for participants to have a crisis of identity during this part of the process, and this is necessary for the process to produce its finest results.

There is a universal western tendency to locate a person solely within the confines of their body. Medicine does this and our minds do it too. But the Phenomenologists are clear that we extend out into the world and have our being as much there as we do in the ontology of our internal experience of selves. Point your finger at an object – your finger extends to include the object in your experience now – you and the object are interconnected without the barrier of the skin limiting your sense of being out-there with in and it being in-here with you. The more evocative the object, the more intense the inner impact of the outer object you get to experience.

So the external environment is somewhere we exist, as well and as much as we do inside our minds and bodies.

However there is another realm in which we exist, and that is further inside our bodies and minds than we are used to admitting.

The mind and body are located between the external environment and **the unconscious mind,** the dark cave from which our unformed source energy comes. We have already said that we call this energy Essence.

We now want to re-establish the unfettered flow and alignment between each of the three realms involved in the journey of pure essence through the mind and body into forms – essence from the unconscious, the conscious mind and the outer world. We do this by reintegrating the Trinity of Essence, Parent and Child. For some of you there may be resonances of myriad other historical trinities, such as the ancient Triple Goddesses of Indo-European religions as much as 10,000 years ago Maiden, Mother, Crone, the Hindu Trimurti, Brahma, Vishnu and Shiva, or Holy Trinity of Christianity, the Father, Son and Holy Spirit. These ancient metaphors are interesting in the light of EMSRP, as indeed is the story of Eden, or flow; eating from the Tree of Knowledge as the separation of the consciously sensate mind from the unconscious source of Essence, and the banishment from the Garden of Eden due to the seduction of the conscious not-me.

Now we must take the deep and significant step into Essence.

Becoming my Essence – Integrating the Trinity.

This process is profound, and marks the integration of the client/participant into their flow as a new and expanding self-concept.

We use a hypnotic induction to conduct this part of the process. It is efficient and achieves powerful results quickly. However, a guided visualization such as has been described earlier can be used equally effectively; it simply takes a little longer.

We present the longer visualization here, but the interactions between the individual parts of the EMSRP Trinity, first parent and child, and then parent and child with essence, will be identical regardless of which relaxation or induction process you decide to use.

Ask the participant to sit comfortably and relax them deeply – or for you hypnotherapists, induce a state of somnambulism, or the deepest state you are able.

The relaxation takes the participant through to a well protected and sheltered garden that is sensually rich and evocative – peaceful sounds of nature in birdsong and flowing water, bright and vivid colours in grass and flowers, the air distinctively scented by flowers, the warmth of the sun palpable.

When you feel sure that the client has become involved in the journey take them towards an area with a garden bench. On the bench allow the child version of them to appear. The client is asked to sit as their nurturing parent next to them in close proximity. Ask them to sense if the child wants to be cuddled or not. Do they want to talk about anything? Tell the parent to act on their intuitions about the child and to feel the feelings that come when they are being the nurturing parent to their inner child. Ask them to talk to them and to listen to their responses.

Then ask them to leave their parent body and enter into the child body, feeling all of the feelings of the child being close to the parent. Ask them if they have anything to say as the child. Ask them to say it to their parent and to allow the parent to answer.

After this interaction is complete ask them to become the parent again. The ask them to notice that someone else is entering the garden. They are about to meet Essence, who is entering now. Use the list from the participant's essence research to describe who they can see in front of them. Ask them to take in who it is they see – what Essence is like, how can they see their power/energy, how does it manifest in them.

Now ask the parent self to move from the child and parent and to enter into Essence – to become them and to look at the parent and child on the bench. Ask them to feel the feelings, and to take note of how the parent and child on the bench seem to them. Ask them to notice what the child most needs from them as Essence – the thing that would most feed them. Ask them to give it to the child now.

Ask them what the parent most needs from them as Essence – the thing that would most feed them. Ask them to give this to them now.

Now suggest that as Essence they put their arms around both parent and child and hold them, and as they hold them to feel both child and parent surrender to the embrace and to slowly slip into their body as essence, to meld with them, to absorb them into the safety of their core physical presence, and to bathe in their pure energy.

At this point simply suggest that they can celebrate their reunion, their perfect harmony. Essence can now flow freely, the child can play and express essence freely, and should they feel anxious, angry or sad, or any other feelings that make them feel inhibited, that Parent Self will listen and do what is needed to smooth the way for Essence and Child to flow again in perfect balance with each other.

Once this is complete, it is time to wake them up – bring them back as the reunited triad.

It is normal for emotional flow during this session in the form of tears; it is important to allow this to happen and express with assurance that this is a good and normal reaction. Participants can often be completely taken aback by their experience. This is a profound moment of experiential insight for the average participant, and so it is important to allow them time to talk through what happened should they so desire, or to take it away to consider it if they choose. Allow them too to express what, if anything at this stage, it meant for them. It is important to allow them to make of it what they make of it without the facilitator interpreting it at any level for them. They are now the parent to themselves.

Assignment.

This is the final assignment.

Take a look at your life audit now that you have *become* your essence. Allow everything to be reviewed without fear, knowing that life is a process and processes are constructed to deliver outcomes. Make two decisions from Essence – two decisions that commit you to aligning significant parts of your life with what you know your Essence is 'for'. Allow this to be as bold as necessary.

END OF SESSION

his final session begins as always with the question "What is different?"

Once this has been mapped and discussed then the focus turns to the assignment.

This is a celebration of the entire process. In this session the participant is invited to make their presentation of their Essence Projects. Once this has been completed and celebrated appropriately.

The facilitator goes through the whole process reminding them of every step and inviting observations from the participant about what they remember about the lessons they learned. The facilitator chooses information from their notes to remind them of the kinds of things they talked about at each step.

Once this is complete, an exit survey form is given to the participant and a final round of data collected using the data form.

A certificate may be presented to them as an EMSRP graduate.

After a fond farewell they are sent on their way with a reminder that in a year they will be asked to complete another data form.

All graduates are invited to join the support forums on our website at www.emsrp.org.

FINAL WORDS.

You now know what EMSRP graduates go through to reawaken their Authentic Selves. It is a process that has profound effects on peoples' lives. It guarantees change. *This is not a process to do alone, to facilitate someone else through without having done every part of it yourself and done a full accreditations training.* This book is written as a full account of the processes and principles of Expressive Meta-Schematic Re-Patterning, and is there as information only, and for the use and reference for qualified and accredited practitioners *only*.

If you wish to do EMSRP as a participant then please contact www.emsrp.org through their website for information regarding accredited and approved practitioners.

If you wish to become an accredited therapist or counsellor then please contact us the same way and we will get back to you.

References

Baars, B.J. (1997) In the Theatre of Consciousness: The Workspace of the Mind, Oxford University Press

Bhel-Chadha G. (1996) 'Basic level and superordinate-like categorical representation early infancy', *Cognition,* vol.60, pp 333-46

Maslow, A. (1943) A Theory of Human Motivation, *Psychological Review,* 50(4), 370–96.

Oatley, K. and Johnson-Baird, P.N. (1987) Towards a Cognitive Theory of Emotions, *Cognition and Emotion,* 1,29-50

Quinn, P.C. and Eimas, P.D., (2000) 'The emergence of category representations during infancy: are separate perceptual and conceptual processes required?' *Journal of Cognition and Development,* vol 1, pp 236-63

Rutter, P. (1990) Sex in the Forbidden Zone, Unwin Paperbacks, London

Wegner, D.M. (2002), *The Illusion of Conscious Will*, Cambridge, Mass., MIT Press.

Wegner, D.M. and Wheatley, T.P. (1999) Apparent mental causation: sources of the experience of will, *American Psychologist,* 54, pp.480-92

Appendix 1: Awareness Form

EMSRP (Expressive Meta-Schematic Re-Patterning) Participant Awareness Declaration.

I acknowledge that I am entering this study with _____ of my own free will. I have had the entire process explained to me and any questions answered to my satisfaction. I do not feel forced or obliged in any way to participate.

I am aware that I can also leave this study of my own free will for whatever reasons and at any time.

I am aware that sessions will cost _____ payable one session in advance and will last from between 1 to 2 hours each. Occasionally we may go over the 2 hours but this is rare.

I am aware that anything I am invited to do in terms of process, conversation or life change assignments I can accept or refuse to do, or postpone until all or any of my questions, doubts or misgivings are fully satisfied. Even then I still have the right to refuse to participate.

Rescheduling sessions will from time to time be necessary and both _____ and I will do our best to give as much notice as possible. There are no financial penalties for changes in scheduling however late.

I am aware that as I progress through this study my circumstances are likely to change. My family and social dynamic are likely to alter and the other parties in the family and social circle may not approve of, understand or even like the changes that occur.

I am aware too that this process assumes that as I change, the status quo in my life will also have to change to accommodate me. This may cause some conflict. I am aware also that the changes may also delight people.

I am choosing to pursue this route because it is my wish to do so, and because I am pursuing solutions to my current life-state which is not agreeable to me at the current time.

I agree that should I experience suicidal fantasies or urges to hurt myself physically and the drive to act on them, I will not act on them, but will seek help from _____ via email at _____. Failing contact with either I will contact the Samaritans on _____. I am aware that they are available 24 hours per day. I am aware that I ultimately hold my destiny in my own hands and after contact with _____ and/or the Samaritans I am master of my own choice.

I am aware that I am bound by a reciprocal agreement of confidentiality and that nothing I reveal to _____ will be revealed to any other party with the exception of _____ own chosen supervisor, in which case my name will be excluded from any discussion. This exception is to facilitate _____ fulfilling his/her professional duty of care in availing him/herself of a qualified second opinion of his own work in supporting me and other

Appendix two: Data Sheet

Completion Stage EMSRP Data Sheet.

Congratulations on graduating from the EMSRP process. Please fill in the form one more time. Thank you.

	SYMPTOM	Score 1-10	
1.	I feel miserable and sad.		I feel that life isn't worth living.
2.	I feel exhausted a lot of the time with no energy.		I have suicidal thoughts.
3.	I feel as if even the smallest tasks are sometimes impossible.		I can see no future.
4.	I comfort eat.		I have feelings of hopelessness.
5.	I am off sex.		I feel irritable or angry more than usual.
6.	I feel very anxious from time to time.		I feel I have no confidence.
7.	I don't want to see people.		I spend a lot of time thinking about what has gone wrong, what will go wrong or what is wrong about me as a person.
8.	Social activity feels impossible.		I feel bad about being critical of others (or even thinking critically about them).
9.	I am scared to be left alone		I feel that life is unfair.
10.	I find it difficult to think clearly.		I have difficulty sleeping or wake up very early in the morning and can't sleep again.
11.	I feel like a failure.		I seem to dream all night long and sometimes have disturbing dreams.
12.	I feel guilty.		I feel that life has/is 'passing me by.'
13.	I feel a burden to others.		I have physical aches and pains which appear to have no physical cause, such as back pain.
			TOTAL TICKS AND SCORE

159

16863956R10090

Printed in Great Britain
by Amazon